# The Anorexic Self

# The Anorexic Self

*A Personal, Political Analysis of a Diagnostic Discourse*

Paula Saukko

State University of New York Press

Published by State University of New York Press, Albany

© 2008 State University of New York

All rights reserved

Printed in the United States of America

No part of this book may be used or reproduced in any manner whatsoever without written permission. No part of this book may be stored in a retrieval system or transmitted in any form or by any means including electronic, electrostatic, magnetic tape, mechanical, photocopying, recording, or otherwise without the prior permission in writing of the publisher.

For information, contact State University of New York Press, Albany, NY
www.sunypress.edu

Production by Marilyn P. Semerad
Marketing by Michael Campochiaro

**Library of Congress Cataloging-in-Publication Data**

Saukko, Paula.
 The anorexic self : a personal, political analysis of a diagnostic discourse / Paula Saukko.
  p. cm.
 Includes bibliographical references and index.
 ISBN 978-0-7914-7461-7 (hardcover : alk. paper) — ISBN 978-0-7914-7462-4 (pbk. : alk. paper)  1. Anorexia nervosa—Social aspects.  2. Feminist theory.  3. Discourse analysis.  I. Title.

RC552.A5S28 2008
362.2'5—dc22

2007032236

10 9 8 7 6 5 4 3 2 1

# Contents

Acknowledgments — vii

1. Introduction: Interrogating the Anorexic Self — 1
2. Rereading the Stories That Became Me: An Autoethnography — 15
3. Fat Boys and Goody Girls: Hilde Bruch's Work on Eating Disorders and the American Ideal of Freedom — 37
4. From Autonomy to Flexibility: News Discourses on Karen Carpenter and Princess Diana — 57
5. Voices and Discourses: Layering Interviews on Eating Disorders — 77
6. From Time-Based Diagnosis to Space-Based Critical Reflection — 99

Notes — 115
References — 117
Index — 129

# Acknowledgments

Most of the research for this book was conducted at the Institute for Communications Research (ICR), University of Illinois, Urbana-Champaign. I am very grateful to the ICR faculty and students for their generous and inspirational intellectual support. This book would not have been written without the encouragement and example of Norman Denzin, and it would have been a very different book without the input of Clifford Christians, C. L. Cole, Larry Grossberg, and Paula Treichler. I also remain grateful to then ICR students, especially Lori Reed, Mary Vavrus, Hua Xu and Mary Walstrom, for their initellectual support and friendship. I am also thankful for Maree Burns, Sarah Riley, Hanna Markula, and Helen Malson for inviting me to the "Weighty Issues" seminar series supported by the British Psychological Association in 2005. I found the discussion and ensuing e-mail exchanges stimulating and helpful in completing this book.

I would also like to warmly thank the women I interviewed for the research that appears in chapter 5 for their time, comments, and friendship.

The research for this book was funded by the Finland-U.S. Educational Commission (The Fullbright Commission), the Graduate College of the University of Illinois, Thanks to Scandinavia Inc., Finnish Cultural Foundation, and George and Ella Ehrnrooth Foundation. I would also like to thank my former colleagues at the Egenis research Centre, University of Exeter, U.K., for supporting me in completing research that did not strictly fall within the ambit of the center.

Some of the material that appears in the chapters of the book has been previously published. I would like to thank Taylor and Francis and National Communication Association (Washington, D.C.) for permission to reprint "Rereading Media and Eating Disorders: Karen Carpenter, Princess Diana and the Healthy Female Self," which appeared in *Critical Studies in Media Communication* 23, no. 2 (2006). I would also like to thank Transaction Publishers/Aldine de Gruyter for permission to reprint parts of "Fat Boys and Goody Girls: Hilde Bruch's Work on Eating Disorders and the American Anxiety About Democracy, 1930–1960," which was published in J. Sobal and

D. Mauer (eds.), *Weighty Issues: The Construction of Fatness and Thinness as Social Problems* (1999). I am also thankful for Elsevier/JAI Press for permission to reprint parts of "Anorexia Nervosa: Rereading Stories That Became Me," which appeared in N. Denzin (ed.), *Cultural Studies, Research Annual* (1996). The latter two articles have been extensively revised for this book.

My usual gratitude extends to my partner Jouni and my son Aksel for putting up with me; I am also thankful for Jouni's excellent editorial comments.

Last, but not least, I am grateful for my acquisitions editor, Jane Bunker, for her support and patience with this book, and the thoughtful and knowledgeable comments of the two anonymous reviewers, which improved the manuscript.

# 1

# *Introduction*
## Interrogating The Anorexic Self

This book has its origins in my personal dissatisfaction with the way in which anorexia is described in psychiatry, the public media, and even in critical feminist analyses. I became anorexic, at the age of 11, three decades ago. I underwent hospitalization, escaped from the hospital (this kind of "premature dropout" has always been a common feature of inpatient treatment of eating disorders, see Halmi et al., 2005), and recovered by my early teens. My memories of active starving are faded. But ever since going through the experience I have felt alienated and insulted by descriptions of what is wrong with anorexics, what psychological and social factors fuel their starving, and what should be done to solve the problem.

As a feminist social scientist I have read many critical studies on social discourses, such as the slender beauty ideal or abhorrence of feminine flesh, which are understood to lie at the root of eating disorders (e.g. Bordo, 1993). I acknowledge the need to critique discourses that invite women to keep their bodies slender, beautiful, and in control. But I have not been mainly frustrated with discourses on thinness. Rather, I have been intellectually troubled and personally insulted by discourses on anorexia, which diagnose anorexic women as having an insufficient self, lacking in autonomy and self-determination, and being vulnerable to outside influences, such as media and peer pressures to be thin (for similar critiques see, Bray, 1996; Malson, 1998; Probyn, 1987) I have been equally uncomfortable with allegations that anorexics have not only taken their femininity too seriously but have also disavowed their gender in a bid to starve their bodies of its womanly shape (e.g., Bordo, 1993; Chernin, 1981). These theories suggest that there is a specific healthy or normal way of embracing one's femininity, or doing gender (Butler, 1990), and that anorexic women, including myself, are not doing it right.

Most feminist research on eating disorders critically analyzes normative discourses on the female body, argued to inform the conditions. In this book I will take these critical analyses one step forward and analyze normative discourses on the female self, delineated in opposition to the disordered anorexic self. In interrogating the discourses I will ask: What kinds of selves and femininities are defined as disordered? What kinds of selves and femininities are defined as "healthy"? What kinds of institutional and political regimes do these psychological ideals support? How are these ideals lived by women who are diagnosed with anorexia? Are there alternative ways of making sense of anorexia that do not reinforce simplified, normative, gendered notions of being?

Recent feminist research has observed that psychiatric discourses that aim to treat women with eating disorders consolidate ideals of strength and fitness similar to those that guide women's starving in the first place (Gremillion, 1992, 2003; Moulding, 2003). I agree with these observations. However, in *The Anorexic Self* I want to critically interrogate not only the content of discourses on eating disorders but also their form.

Research on eating disorders is often grounded on a dichotomous way of conceptualizing their personal implications, such as false consciousness versus emancipation, and their political dimensions, such as dominance versus freedom. This type of reasoning mimics and fuels anorexic thinking in terms of one-dimensional absolutes. I contend that discourses that inform anorexia, such as idealization of female thinness or success, have both empowering and disempowering elements. Research that does not acknowledge these contradictions ends up presenting anorexics as victims of sexist discourses and oversimplifying the personal and political agendas embedded in the ideals.

When exploring the discourses used to diagnose and treat eating disorders I do not want to repeat the problems evident in critical analyses of discourses that inform the conditions. My aim is not to simply "denounce" the diagnostic and popular notions of anorexia. Drawing on dialogic theory (Bakhtin, 1981; Volosinov, 1973) I explore the personal implications of discourses on eating disorders in terms of contradictory social voices or accents, which often pull women in different directions and can be experienced as either healing or humiliating. I also study the politics embedded in discourses on anorexia not in terms of systemic medical/sexist dominance but as emanating from complex social struggles (Jasanoff, 2004; Marcus, 1998). Studying the personal and political together allows me to explore how the social struggles articulated by discourses on eating disorders translate into and are negotiated in the anorexic woman's intrapersonal contestations.

In the chapters that follow I will explore how discourses on eating disorders acquire diverse meaning and have different implications in the personal lives of women who have had eating disorders. I will also investigate the evolving and contradictory social and political agendas that have structured clinical, popular, and feminist discourses on eating disorders, from the postwar concerns over "feminine" mass culture to the present idealization of female adaptability. By illuminating the many sides of the discourses I work against the grain of absolutist anorexic thinking in terms of either good or bad and hope to cultivate an open-minded, critically self-reflective attitude toward all discourses that invite us to become who we want to be.

But before embarking on this project it is useful to locate the book within the wider body of literature on anorexia.

## Research on Eating Disorders

There is a vast clinical literature on the etiology and treatment of anorexia, spanning from the nineteenth century to the present (see Brumberg, 1988). *The Anorexic Self* discusses some of the main clinical theories, but it belongs to culturally and socially orientated critical feminist literature that focuses on social discourses that shape the experience of anorexia and how we make sense of it.

Feminist research on anorexia begun to flourish in the 1970s and the 1980s. At the time the disorder was becoming more prevalent and it attracted professional and lay attention. The third edition of the American Psychiatric Association's *Diagnostic and Statistical Manual* (DSM-III), published in 1980, provided, for the first time, a detailed description of anorexia nervosa. Popular interest in anorexia was sparked by the death of the soft-rock singer Karen Carpenter from complications of anorexia in 1983. The higher incidence of anorexia coincided with the second wave of feminism, and the early feminist writers on anorexia (e.g., Chernin, 1981; Orbach, 1986), as well as some psychiatrists (Bruch, 1978), interpreted the condition to articulate the contradictory demands placed upon women to both continue to suppress their own needs and please others and to move forward to become individuals of achievement in their own right. Feminist scholarship pointed out that the slender female body communicated both of these demands. For example, Bordo (1993) insightfully discussed how images of women in business suits or engaging in various fitness activities reinforced the liberal feminist and individualist ideology that women could do everything that men could do. This liberal feminist ethos was associated with a fit and thin androgynous body shape. At the same time, Bordo pointed out, the slender body also echoed the old ideal of a frail and self-effacing femininity.

Feminist analyses of anorexia emphasized the role of gendered societal norms and developments in the etiology of eating disorders. Investigating social factors made good sense against the fact that approximately ninety percent of anorexics were women, and that the condition was becoming increasingly common at a particular historical conjuncture. It was also observed that, at least initially, anorexics tended to come from well-to-do, white, middle-class families, as the new pressures for women to achieve were most acutely felt among this social stratum.

Feminists gave a decidedly gendered and political spin to eating disorders, but their theories also overlapped with and borrowed from psychiatric explanations. Both psychiatry and feminism concluded that anorexia articulates women's (feminine) inability to live up to the ideal, healthy (masculine) autonomous or independent self. Feminist discussion on how anorexia embodies women's attempts to suppress their gendered body also resonated with the psychiatric interpretation of anorexia as indicating a gender identity disorder (for recent experiments testing this old hypothesis see Hepp, Spindler, & Milos, 2005 and Johnson, Brems, & Fischer, 1996). Psychiatry has viewed anorexics' lack of autonomy or their gender identity problems as caused by a psychological weakness specific to individual women. Feminists have argued that troubles relating to self-determination and gender identity affect all women in sexist societies, with anorexics simply representing the gravest end of the continuum. Psychiatry and feminism agreed that the remedy to anorexia is to enable women to "graduate" into independent selfhood, even if the former has suggested personal reform and the latter has proposed political reform as a means to this end.

The feminist and psychiatric theories on anorexia have provided many insights on the condition. However, the intertwining of feminist and psychiatric notions of anorexia has meant that for a long time diagnostic discourses on anorexia were taken as "true" representations of the condition. An early project that provided a more contextual interpretation of theories of eating disorders was Brumberg's (1988) analysis of the emergence of anorexia nervosa as a mental disorder. She argued that the nineteenth-century psychiatric definitions of women's starving in terms of anorexia nervosa bore witness to the receding of religious authority, which had defined women's starving in terms of religious miracles and chastity, and the increasing dominance of the scientific worldview. Thus, the seeming irrationality of the "fasting girls" became the counterpole and object of investigation for the male-identified rationality of the Enlightenment psychiatric science (Hepworth, 1999).

Critical feminist interest in discourses on anorexia increased in the 1990s. Scholars started to investigate not only meanings women associated with their starving but also meanings that women associated with having anorexia. This research drew attention to the way in which anorexics were often insulted and alienated by descriptions of the condition (Malson, 1998; Malson et al., 2004; Rich, 2006), a fact that has also become apparent in the controversial and contradictory "pro-ana" Web sites where women with eating disorders have defended their "right" to starve (Fox, Ward, & O'Rourke, 2005; Mulveen & Hepworth, 2006; Pollack, 2003). Some have argued that discussions on anorexia frequently attribute anorexia to female irrationality, and that this was manifest in historical psychiatric works as well as contemporary health professionals' speech (Hepworth, 1999). Others contended that discourses on beauty ideals and anorexia framed women as "bimbos," unusually vulnerable to mass-mediated images of slenderness (Bray, 1996; Probyn, 1987). It was also suggested that the focus on middle-class high-achieving women's struggle with self-determination was oblivious of issues such as sexual abuse (Wooley, 1994), racism, poverty, and heterosexism (Thompson, 1994) that other groups of women associated with their troubled eating. Perhaps most importantly, it was pointed out that discourses on anorexia and lack of autonomy ended up consolidating similar normative ideals of strength, independence, and control over the female body that often informed the anorexic's starving in the first place (Gremillion, 1992, 2003; McNeill, 1993; Moulding, 2003). As such, the discourses that precipitated eating disorders and the discourses that explained and treated the disorders seemed to move in a vicious circle, affirming similar historical, social ideals that accounted for women's excruciating attempts to conquer their gender.

*The Anorexic Self* draws on and contributes to this critical feminist research. It identifies with the "second wave" of feminist research on eating disorders, which has begun to critically interrogate the submerged gendered agendas embedded in discourses on the disorders themselves. I agree with the observations of critical feminists (Gremillion, 1992, 2003; McNeill, 1993; Moulding, 2003) that discourses on anorexia often affirm historical, normative notions of traditional femininity as deficient and a fit or strong femininity as ideal—notions similar to those that fuel eating disorders in the first place. This book takes these observations forward in two respects. First, it offers a series of case studies that explores the personal implications of discourses on eating disorders for women diagnosed with anorexia and bulimia and that investigates the varied social and political agendas and struggles that discourses on eating disorders articulate in psychiatry and public media. Second, it develops and applies a methodological and conceptual framework that is sensitive to the ambivalences and many sides, including healing, humiliating, progressive and reactionary, of the discourses on eating disorders. It is my hope that this framework will foster an anti-anorexic, less simplistically judgmental, and more critically self-reflective way through which we can relate to our selves, the people we study, and the societies in which we live.

## Methodological Considerations

The methodological and conceptual framework that underpins this book considers the personal and political dimensions of eating disorders differently. I work against the classical interpretation of the personal experience of anorexics as being "outside of the true," as either disordered (in psychiatry) or under false consciousness (in feminism). These ideas have contributed to one-dimensional normativity in much research on eating disorders and have also been conducive of disrespectful ways of treating anorexics in clinical practice and research. Recent research has discovered that the internal world of an anorexic is much more complex than the dichotomous theories propose, and anorexics are often aware of the both thrilling and damaging nature of their starving and that they are also aware of the problematic nature of discourses on anorexia, which describe them as vain or spoilt (see Malson, 1998; Rich, 2006).

Following Volosinov (1973), I conceptualize the consciousness of anorexic women not as false or true but as always polyvocal "internal speech," or dialogues between multiple voices. The voices are not personal but echo the various social "accents" or agendas and sensibilities of their times. For example, anorexics' starving is often underpinned by a desire to be strong and successful. This has been dismissed as feminine frustration with not being able to be truly strong and independent (Bruch, 1978) or interpreted as succumbing to a male-defined dominant ideology (Bordo, 1993). Both of these interpretations are strongly normative, either upholding or denouncing the ideal of strength. Dialogic theory facilitates an analysis of the issue in a way that does not affirm or reject the ideal of strength but pays attention to the many voices that speak through it, or its "multi-accentuality" (Volosinov, 1973, also Hermans & Kempen, 1993, from a narrative therapy perspective). So, the anorexic pursuit of strength can be seen to testify *both* for the empowering possibilities embedded in discourses that invite women to be strong and successful *and* for the personal disempowerment that may ensue if these desires begin to dominate women's lives or the social disempowerment that results from consolidating structures of inequality based on individual competitiveness. Similarly, many diagnostic discourses on anorexia can be interpreted not as right or wrong or helpful or detrimental but as often both empowering and disempowering as will be discussed later in the book.

Dialogic theory helps to make sense of anorexics' starving not in stigmatizing terms of being a "dope" but through communicating about many contradictory ideals, which are not necessarily all reactionary or sexist. It also facilitates a critical analysis of the both helpful and hurtful personal implications of discourses that claim to treat or emancipate anorexics. Moreover, it underlines that we are always only partially aware of all the many discourses and voices that inform our thoughts or actions or, to draw on Foucault (1982), we are always both active subjects and acted upon objects in relation to discourses that shape our consciouness. This means that not only women with eating disorders but also researchers are both enabled and blinded by discourses. In this spirit this book aims to conduct research on women with eating disorders in a less diagnostic and more egalitarian or mutually critically reflective manner.

Analysis shows, too, that the political dimension of eating disorders has also been underpinned by dichotomies. Research may have acknowledged how, in a contradictory manner, discourses on thinness both negate and affirm femininity (Bordo, 1993). Regardless, these works tend to interpret discourses on thinness and fitness as simply dominant (Bordo, 1993; Gremillion, 2003).

The trouble with this type of research is that it understands dominance in relation to an abstract "system," such as sexism, capitalism, or neoliberalism. This makes the research blind to the complexity of discourses defined as dominant and to the problems embedded in positions defined as emancipatory. In this book I do not examine politics in relation to anorexia in such abstract terms. Rather, I seek to examine how specific discourses on anorexia dominate or resist very particular, contingent, contextual social and political agendas in a given time and place (Saukko, 2003, pp. 39–54).

For example, postwar theories of anorexia as symptomatic of mass culture attacked the complacent, conservative, and increasingly wealthy middle-class lifestyle and the domesticated femininity associated with it. While these theories resisted 1950s conservatism and sexism, they also articulated a masculinist, intellectualist, dominant disdain towards the feminine private sphere (Felski, 1995; Huyssen, 1986). Mass culture theories not only supported the left-liberal agendas of the Frankfurt school (Adorno & Horkheimer, 1979) but also fueled conservative fears about communism and the demise of American individualism.

Attentiveness to multiple political dimensions in discourses in which anorexics are seen as victims of mass culture brings into relief how these discourses can simultaneously support progressive, feminist, reactionary, and sexist politics. It also makes it intelligible why discourses on eating disorders can be personally experienced as helpful and humiliating at the same time, as the social struggles embedded in the discourses translate into intrapersonal contradictions and contestations. The complexity of social agendas embedded in discourses on eating disorders calls for a more nuanced feminist engagement with the politics surrounding the condition. It draws critical attention to discourses that are deemed to be counter-hegemonic or emancipatory, such as critiques of consumer culture, and to discourses that seem fresh and new, such as the emergent ideal of "feminine" adaptability and openness to the world in contemporary psychiatry, pop psychology, and management theory.

## Structure of the Book

To examine the various personal and political implications of discourses on anorexia, this book is structured around empirical case studies that focus on a specific "site" where eating disorders are an issue. This research strategy is informed by Marcus's (1998) heuristic of "multi-sited ethnography." Marcus's work is grounded in anthropology, and he criticizes the discipline's tendency to juxtapose a local lifeworld and a global system, which ends up a "theoretically constituted holistic frame that gives context to the study of local subjects" (pp. 80–81). I contend that this is what happens in much research on eating disorders, which presupposes a sexist system, manifesting itself in the thin body ideal, imposed on individual women.

Multi-sited ethnography does not presuppose a system but considers the object of study as "an emergent object," which takes shape and transforms across many contexts or sites. In this book I aim to map some of the contours of the discourse on anorexia, which emerges and takes shape across multiple social sites. I have selected a few sites for close inspection based on a broad review of psychiatric, popular, and feminist discourses on eating disorders.

The sites studied capture key moments, institutions, individuals, and groups that have galvanized discussion on eating disorders. I focus on classic accounts of anorexia—such as media coverage of Karen Carpenter's anorexia or stories of white, middle-class women who have had anorexia—in order to problematize them. In these accounts I show that what we take for granted about eating disorders is shaped by historical contingencies, does not necessarily fit with lived experiences, and produces troubling political and psychological implications.

In addition to investigating easily recognizable cases I have also aimed to cover a diversity of discourses in terms of historical period (from 1930s to the present day), different institutions and genres (psychiatry and news media), spheres of life (political developments, personal experience), and locations (the United States, the United Kingdom, Finland). Exploring discourses on anorexia at different times and in different places brings into relief the idiosyncrasies and contingencies of various explanations and highlights the varied social and political agendas that anorexia is harnessed to support. Studying both the historical and political production of discourses on anorexia and lived experiences of the discourses illuminates the important interaction between the political and the personal.

The first site to be examined, in chapter 2, is my own personal experience of anorexia at the age of eleven. The chapter is an introspective account, interspersed with excerpts from my hospital records, and discusses my treatment with behavior modification, which consisted of strict regulation of my eating, movement, schedule, and personal contacts. I describe the haunted feeling of being put into the middle of a prison-like regime that closely resembled my anorexic behavior and my escape from the hospital. I feared I would completely lose my mind, which was interpreted as possibly requiring my rediagnosis as psychotic rather than neurotic. I also discuss how, after recovery, I encountered and tried to make sense of the popular discourses on anorexia as related to beauty ideals, perfectionism, and disturbed gender identity. The aim of the autoethnography is not to present my "true" story of anorexia against the incorrect medical and popular understandings, but rather to address the fact that my experience is only accessible to me through the discourses on eating disorders, which I have both violently resisted and incorporated into my self-image. I seek to illuminate, from the inside out, the occasionally illuminative but also limiting and misguiding effects that psychiatric and public discourses on anorexia had for my treatment and self-understanding, particularly in a situation where, because I was a child diagnosed with a mental disorder, my protests about the way in which I was defined and treated fell on deaf ears.

In chapter 3 I investigate the historical origins of the classical notion of the anorexic woman as an insufficiently autonomous "goody" girl fallen victim to media and parental pressures to be pretty and to achieve. This notion shaped my treatment. The chapter focuses on the world-known psychiatrist Hilde Bruch's pioneering work on autonomy and obesity and anorexia. Bruch's work on obesity in the 1930s focused on poor immigrant children, and she argued their obesity was precipitated by the authoritarian and traditional cultures of their families, most of which had recently immigrated from Eastern Europe. Bruch's theory on the cultural and social origins of obesity contradicted the prevailing eugenic notion of fatness as indicating an inherent or racial physical and mental disposition. Yet, it still reiterated that recent immigrants posed a threat to American values and the political system; Bruch relocated the threat from the immigrant families' genes to their culture.

Bruch's postwar research on anorexia focused on a very different social group: affluent, middle-class young girls. In this case, Bruch argued that the women began starving in order to assert their own will, having been trained to be overly docile by their overpowering suburban mothers. Bruch's criticism of middle-class mothering and the suburban culture of the 1950s and 1960s attacked the conservative complacency and domesticated femininity of Cold War America. Yet her theory also read eating disorders through the lens of mass culture, which was feared to breed fascism and communism and was often associated with the private sphere of female reproduction and consumption. Thus, Bruch interpreted both the immigrant children's obesity and the middle-class girls' starving in relation to contemporary American agonies about democracy and its threats, such as Eastern European traditionalism or suburban feminine conformism. What the chapter on Bruch demonstrates is that our current understanding of obesity and anorexia as having to do with lack of autonomous self-will does not indicate a psychological universal but is deeply lodged in a specific historical place and time and its political agenda.

In chapter 4 I explore later articulations of anorexia and bulimia through an examination of the news representation of the two most famous women with eating disorders: Karen Carpenter and Princess Diana. After Carpenter's death of complications of anorexia in 1983, U.S. and U.K. news media both eulogized her dreamy, wholesome, and phenomenally successful soft rock and deplored her as a nonautonomous female, who fell victim to the suburban culture and the conservative American family values of the 1970s that her music seemed to epitomize. Most news media represented Princess Diana as the British New Labour woman, flexible and self-transforming, who graduated from a virgin princess to an outspoken yet caring divorcée charitable towards ethnic minorities and people with HIV. The conservative news media framed her as a classical female hysteric slashing herself with penknives and throwing herself down the stairs in front of a helpless husband.

What these both different and similar media representations witness is that eating disorders are mobilized to tell moral stories about ideal femininity and good society that fit the zeitgeist of a particular moment, such as the 1980s neoconservative United States or the 1990s New Labour Britain. These news narratives also tell about the contradictory nature of popular discourses on anorexia. Carpenter's death, for example, is mobilized to reveal the dark psychological and political underside of the neoconservative politics of the 1980s while, at the same time, it is used to associate her femininity and softness with regressive personality and reactionary politics.

Chapter 5 returns to the personal experience of anorexia. In it, interviews with four women who have had anorexia or bulimia are discussed. The interviews were conducted using a critically self-reflexive or "layered" methodology that is attentive to both women's stories or voices and discourses that interlace the voices. In this spirit, I asked each woman interviewed to both tell her story about her experience of an eating disorder and, afterwards, to evaluate discourses that have defined eating disorders. The stories of the women highlighted that even though many of them had pursued familiar aims of thinness and success while starving or bingeing and purging, their goals were not uniform, nor could they be interpreted as just being informed by sexist or reactionary ideologies. The women's reflections on discourses on anorexia and bulimia were very varied; some thought the descriptions were true and illuminating, even if they felt "stupid" about having had anorexia, others were acutely critical of the discourses for repeating notions of women's weakness, similar to those that had originally fueled their starving. However, all the women, who had each recovered from an eating disorder, shared a life philosophy that was ambivalent about all (therapeutic, marketing, sports, political, feminist, and vegetarian) discourses that invited them to imagine themselves in a specific way. The chapter concludes with suggesting that research has much to learn from the women's critically self-reflective approach to a wide range of discourses.

The last chapter, chapter 6, continues the task begun in this introduction: to develop a different conceptual and methodological approach to eating disorders. It discusses the possibilities as well as problems for understanding anorexic consciousness embedded in recent work on narrative therapy (Epston & White, 1990; Hermans & Kempen, 1993; Maisel, Epston, & Borden. 2004). Drawing on science and technology studies (Jasanoff, 2004) and multi-sited ethnography (Marcus, 1998), the chapter outlines a way of studying the political dimension of eating disorders that understands politics as a heterogenous social struggle. The chapter argues that research on eating disorders has typically followed a time-based logic in terms of linear development from sickness to health and from oppression to emancipation. It suggests the use of a space-based approach, which views consciousness as consisting of multiple voices that exist side by side and in conversation with each other, as if in space rather than hierarchically in time. These intrapersonal conversations and contestations echo political issues of their times, which are viewed in terms of contradictory social struggles rather than a dominant ideology. This approach helps the researcher to see that personal and political life is more complicated it seems. It also highlights that trying to resolve personal or political contradictions by adamantly pursuing one goal and agenda may cause significant damage, as witnessed by eating disorders and many global developments of our time, and that addressing complexities and ambivalences will be conducive of a more balanced psyche and polity even if it seems less straightforward.

## Note on Interpreting and Writing

Before moving on to the "real" analysis, a few words are in order on the interpretation and writing that structure the book. The analyses presented in the chapters that follow are based on diverse material, and different methods and genres of writing are applied in the different analyses.

Bakhtin, among others, has noted that different languages do not simply reflect realities but refract them, partly producing different realities (Bakhtin, 1981; also Haraway, 1997). Richardson (2000; Richardson & St. Pierre, 2005) has similarly argued that different methods and genres of writing allow us to look at the world from different angles. She rationalizes the use of different perspectives by giving a different spin to the classical social scientific method of triangulating. According to the classical definition, triangulating between different methods and materials aims to increase the validity of the research in terms of enhancing its truthfulness, as if using multiple lenses would yield a more accurate image of the research object. Richardson defines triangulation as looking at the world through different angles of a prism, which will always cast the phenomenon studied into a different light.

This book seeks to capture different discourses on anorexia and reflect on their multiple dimensions. Capturing this multiplicity requires different methodologies and writing genres, as well as an innovative framework to bring the different angles together both within and between different chapters. In chapter 2 I use critical autoethnography (e.g., Bordowitz, 1994; Minh-Ha, 1989) both to convey my experience of anorexia and to critically interrogate the social discourses that have made my experience intelligible for me. In chapter 3 I use traditional social historical research method and prose to examine Hilde Bruch's research on eating disorders, and in chapter 4 I employ discourse-analytic methods to make sense of the complexities of news coverage of Karen Carpenter and Princess Diana. In chapter 5 I use a self-reflective interview technique and a "layered" mode of writing (Ronai, 1998) to discuss how women who have had eating disorders both internalize and criticize different aspects of discourses on eating disorders to make sense of themselves and their lives. The last chapter, like this introduction, uses more or less traditional academic argumentation and writing.

Different chapters of *The Anorexic Self* also convey different authorial positions. An autoethnographic style posits the author as making a personal confession, as well as critically reflecting on her confession (on this see Bordowitz, 1994), whereas traditional historical analysis conveys detached authority. My use of self-reflective and, on occasion, personal style of writing is a response to the debates that have criticized the use and abuse of traditional scientific authority and accompanying objectivist narration (see Clifford & Marcus, 1986). Still, by using different genres of writing in the different chapters I seek to occupy personal, self-reflective and scientific/authoritative subject positions and to unsettle the often reified expectations of feminine personableness and masculine expertise.

By shifting between different methods, genres, times, places, and authorial positions, I hope to unsettle reified views on anorexia by illustrating that there are many ways of interpreting the condition and that these interpretations produce a variety of personal and political implications. I also seek to create a book that embodies a different, less one-eyed or anorexic, and more open-ended and multiperspectival way of approaching eating disorders, psychological health, and politics.

# 2

## Rereading the Stories That Became Me
### An Autoethnography

It is 1975 in Helsinki, Finland. I escaped from the hospital. I took the back elevator they used for bringing food to the floor. I ran frantically across the hospital lawn to a tram that was passing by. In the tram I realized my psychiatrist was sitting in the front. She did not see me. I got off at the next stop and ran through the streets and parks without stopping. I was going home. When I arrived at home, my mother and father were having traditional Finnish afternoon coffee with sweet bread ("pulla"). I promised my parents that I would start eating if they would not return me to the hospital but would allow me to stay at home. To prove my point I ate a piece of sweet bread.

My mother called the hospital and told them I had arrived home. "Yes, yes, but . . . ," I overheard her saying on the phone. My doctor decided that they would not send an ambulance to bring me back by force, because it could reverse my "positive development." I could stay home for the weekend. On Monday my mother called the hospital and told them I was not

---

This chapter is reprinted from *Cultural Studies, Research Annual*, N. Denzin (ed.) "Anorexia Nervosa: Reading Stories That Became Me," 1996, with permission from Elsevier. The original was extensively revised for this book.

returning. They demanded that she and my father sign a statement whereby they would take full responsibility for whatever happened to me, including death. My parents signed the statement.

This scene took place thirty years ago when I was eleven years old. When I initiated my study on anorexia, I decided to look at my experience from the other side of the fence and requested to see my hospital records, stored in the Finnish Central Hospital Archive. According to the Data Protection Law I had the right to see my file, but the law had a caveat: individuals considered incompetent or potentially harmed by reading their files would be excluded from this right to retrieve their data. As I had been diagnosed mentally disordered, and by default possibly incompetent and vulnerable to harm, I had to make some additional phone calls. I was told my records would be sent back to the Aurora Children's Hospital where I had been hospitalized, and I could read them there. A doctor was supposed to be present to explain the contents of the file to me but—for better or worse—she was too busy. I was allowed to photocopy the contents of the thick file, but a young man watched over me to make sure I did not snatch any of the original papers. I leafed through the sheets of paper, turned yellow by the decades, and paused at September 29, 1975—the date of my self-initiated discharge. At the bottom of my "decursus," or brief description of the development of the illness, my psychiatrist had concluded: *Clearly loosing her sense of reality. Becomes tremendously anxious, when cannot control and rule the situation. We will let go in order to avoid psychotic development. A psychosis-level condition could lie at the root of all problems?*

I stared at the record and a torrent of surreal memories flooded into my mind. Memories of being continuously monitored and of having judgments passed on everything I did and said in terms of what each "really" meant. My own interpretations of my thoughts and actions and the medical staff's interpretation of them were often at loggerheads with each other. I had escaped from the hospital thinking I would lose my mind if I stayed there much longer. I felt I should be allowed go in order to avoid a descent deeper into the depths of insanity. My psychiatrist concluded, however, that my escape was proof that my condition might not be underpinned by a neurosis but a full-blown madness or psychosis. So while we concurred that it would not be beneficial to make me stay, that conclusion was based on very different ideas.

A friend of mine, a psychologist, interpreted the coded language of the note to me, saying that standard psychological theory argues that individuals develop neurotic symptoms as a defensive reaction in order to shield their fragile egos. If one too abruptly deprives the patient of these protective symptoms, such as starving, their egos may disintegrate, precipitating a psychosis. This may be the standard psychological explanation. However, by positioning me as if teetering on the brink of psychosis both before and after my escape, my psychiatrist located all insanity in me—not in the hospital environment, from which I had escaped in abject panic.

In this chapter I reread the diagnostic discourse, which defined me as psychotic, through my autobiographical experience. Autobiographic writing often aims to capture, to quote Norman Denzin, "the wild beast of lived experience," but is often oblivious of the fact that "no one exists outside a text and that texts produce subjects" (Denzin, 1992, 27). I am mindful that experiences do not emerge out of "wild" consciousness. There is no genuine anorexic experience to be discovered under the rubble of decades of diagnostic treatments and explanations, and searching for the wild or real anorexic experience can easily become a form of self-diagnosis where internalized psychiatric theories are rehashed and represented as authentic voices of the subaltern. The starting point of my autobiography is that my experience of anorexia is only accessible to me through the diagnostic discourse—or that there is no anorexic me outside of these stories that have become me.

Following Foucault, I view this chapter as a "critical ontology of the self," which is a *critique* of what we are," and which "is at one and the same time the historical analysis of the limits that are imposed on us and an *experiment* with the possibility of going beyond them" (Foucault, 1984a, p. 50, emphasis added). Thus, I will use introspection to explore discourses on anorexia, which often seem emancipatory from the surface, not to suggest my account of anorexia is "truer" than medical explanations, but to highlight the rarely explored disempowering underside of diagnostic discourses that define and treat eating disorders. At the same time, this chapter is also an experiment in that in it, I attempt to develop a mode of self-reflective autoethnographic writing that goes against the diagnostic logic.

## *The Modification*

Anorexia nervosa has been defined as the crystallization of our times (Bordo, 1993), however, scholars have traced women's starving to at least the female medieval saints in Western history (Bunym, 1987). In different times, women's fasting has had different meanings. Still in the nineteenth century (and sometimes also now, see Giles Banks, 1992) fasting women were understood by themselves and their "audiences" in terms of religious miracles, purity, and chastity (Brumberg, 1988).

I first heard the name anorexia nervosa when the epithet "nervosa" appeared in my papers at the hospital after my initial diagnosis "anorexia," or loss of appetite. As documented by my medical records, my diagnosis was easy: *A thin girl with thick brown hair and with her shoulders hunched up is received. In the examinations a normal finding in the EEG. Stomach x-ray, normal finding. Skull x-ray, normal finding. In the psychological examinations the picture matches perfectly to anorexia nervosa.* I did not fully understand what they were doing to me at the hospital, and it was never explained. Yet, the questions (there were never answers), practices, and underlying assumptions molded me. When I read the modern psychiatric core narratives of anorexia nervosa from the 1970s, I feel like I am reading the table of contents of my self-understanding. Among the psychiatric descriptions are theories that I had violently rejected, while there are others that I have interwoven into my sense of self without being able to recall their origin. According to the definitions of anorexia from the 1970s—and the descriptions have changed little since—it allegedly has to do with adolescence; (lack of) sexuality; fear of mature (normal) womanhood; dysfunctional family (dominant and "intrusive" mother, passive or "ineffectual" father); perfectionism; shyness; introvertedness; distorted body image; thin beauty ideal; and, perhaps, some failure in the hypothalamus gland (for a review, see, e.g., Bemis, 1978).

I stopped eating during the summer of 1975. Why? I don't know. I have scattered summer memories. I am at my mother's friend's summer cottage. I am supposed to keep company with their spoiled and chubby girl who is my age. She has white hair and pinkish skin. They try to make me eat as much as her. Pigs. I decide to make sure I am not gaining weight. Later that summer we go to Lapland with my father to visit his brother/cousin Ilmo's widow and her children. Ilmo had committed suicide a few years earlier by shooting himself in the mouth with a shotgun. He was really my father's cousin, but throughout my father's childhood his mother kept abandoning him to foster homes and to orphanages and frequently left him with her sister, Ilmo's mother. Ilmo and my father grew up together as brothers. It rains incessantly, and we sit in the bedroom with Ilmo's two youngest daughters and talk. The night when Ilmo shot himself, they tell me in a dark voice, he had come to look for his youngest daughters, because he had wanted to take them with him. Blood in the fields. He had seven children. How do they live? Nobody works here. We babysit the one-year-old daughter of one of my older cousins, who is working somewhere in the south. The little girl's older sister is spending the holidays with their father, but he has not taken the younger one with him, arguing she is not his biological child. My father and the other adults go boozing as always. Why? The family history. The Finnish Civil War, 1917–1918. The working and landless poor form a "red army," backed by

Russian revolutionaries, and rise up against the whites, backed up by the Germans. Russia transforms into the Soviet Union, experiencing a short period of revolutionary euphoria under Lenin before Stalin's state terrorism takes over. In Finland the reds loose. They end up in prison camps and die by the tens of thousands. My great grandfather, who had been a member of the red army, escapes across the northern border to Russia. When he visits his family, the counterinsurgency tracks him down and captures him just across the border on the Russian side and executes him. My great grandmother abandons the children in order to remarry. She leaves three orphan girls; one of them is my eight-year-old grandmother. Odd jobs. Odd men. We are the offspring. Offspring of poverty, exploitation, desperation, and irresponsibility. I stop eating.

Back to Helsinki. I run. I hate running. I run until I taste the blood in my mouth. My throat and my lungs hurt, my heart beats wildly. I get up from the Olympic-size pool at the stadium where the games were held in 1952. I tremble; I am exhausted and cold. I take a shower. A strange ecstatic feeling invades my body; I am light, warm, and excited. The starvation high, I know now. I don't even drink water. I enter the anorexic world known from the many autobiographies written by anorexics. What were your inner feelings, someone asked just recently. None. Much later I attend a lecture on body image at a large American Midwest university. An anorectic girl speaks. "I used to be able to see the sky and think it's beautiful and everything, and now I just think about food," she says. Her eyes fill with tears. So do mine.

My mother gets frantic. What's the matter with you? I have lost twenty pounds in three weeks. She rushes me to a doctor, who ignores my mother. The second doctor sends me to a hospital. I am hospitalized right away. I have a record. I had stayed at the hospital the year before because of mysterious stomachaches.

Anorexia nervosa has been treated with different kinds of methods, such as drugs, electroconvulsive therapy, family and individual therapy, and psychoanalysis. Reading my experience against the psychiatric literature I can see (I was never told) that I was mostly treated with "behavior modification." This therapy was especially popular in the 1970s, although it is still often used in combination with other therapies. In behavior modification, simple stimulus-response techniques are used in an attempt to modify the patient's behavior. The anorexic is rewarded with positive "reinforcements" when she eats and negative reinforcements when she refuses to eat. If the patient doesn't eat she can be tube fed, isolated, or ordered to bed rest; some therapists have even gone so far as to forbid the patient to get up to go to the bathroom. Visits, mail, or television may be prohibited. If the patient eats, she is gradually allowed to have visits or to do something she likes, such as physical exercise (e.g., Garfinkel, Kline, & Stancer, 1973; Halmi, Powers, & Cunningham, 1973).

After the diagnosis they tighten my program. I am made to eat alone in my room. A nurse watches me. She reads women's magazines. I take the yogurt cup's lid off without licking it. Carefully I scoop the yogurt without touching the edges with my spoon so that a maximum amount of yogurt clings to the edges. My weight is measured every morning. At first they take a blood test from me three times a day, then once; a urine test is taken every week. They make me defecate with a diuretic twice a week, on Tuesdays and Fridays. They tell me that if I continue not eating, I will no longer be able to digest food. I will become sterile. If I don't eat, they will feed me. Probably intravenously.

They start giving me Largactil®, an antipsychotic medication. I am not getting better: I have been caught in the bathroom doing push-ups. Largactil—I learn from the Internet—is considered a "major tranquilizer." Chlorpromazine, the active compound in the medication, "works by blocking a variety of receptors in the brain, particularly dopamine receptors, and this prevents the overactivity of dopamine in the brain" (netdoctor.co.uk, 2007). I have to take the pill four times a day; they wake me up at three in the morning to take one. The pills make me unable to think, to sleep, or to stay awake. Before them I had walked steadily from one end of the hall to the other. To exercise. After the pills I do not have the strength. I just lay on the bed. Major tranquilizer.

My parents are allowed to visit me two hours a week. The doctor explains they can split the two hours whichever way they want. They can visit me twice a week for an hour or eight times a week for fifteen minutes. As long as it is two hours. If you eat, you can see your parents more. If you eat, you can take small trips outside of the hospital. You can even go running. Running? But I hate running. I only run because this horrible condition makes me run. How did it ever occur to them to "reward" me by allowing me to run?

My regime against their regime. Gremillion (1992, 2003) has pointed out that psychiatry ends up as an accomplice to the same cruel sociocultural processes that inform anorexia. It fights its patients with their own method, control, deepening it. I was even disorganized in my regime. I just ran and refused all food and liquids. I had been curious about calories and grams, but my life starts revolving around them at the hospital. I try to outrun them. The push-ups. The yogurt. But they are relentless, and very organized. Weighing. Blood test. Urine test. Eight times fifteen minutes. Two thousand calories. Breakfast at nine. Lunch at twelve. Snack at two.

Dinner at five. Evening snack at eight. The tablets every six hours. Tuesday, Friday, defecation days. I wake up every night at three a.m., which is probably not in the program. I can't sleep nor can I stay awake. The tablets confuse me. I can't think. The rites break my day. I eat diet ice cream without any good or bad feelings. I have no choice. Their regime is stronger. It breaks mine.

Other patients. There is a boy who has had polio. Once his father shows me his second-grade picture. A round-faced brown-haired boy. Now he is fifteen. He also had been there the year before. Then he could utter some simple words, now he only sits crooked in his wheelchair and roars during the nights. The "fats" (children who are hospitalized to lose weight) eat 1300 calories a day. A fat boy always jokes and looks at my pancakes licking his lips. I like him.

I have a session with the psychiatrist once a week. Every time I hope it will help me somehow. She slowly asks me questions. Once she lights a cigarette. Silently she blows the smoke at me. She smokes Kents. Do you feel like a rubber band that has to stretch to the maximum to keep your parents together? Yes. Can you think of a way to help your (alcoholic) father? I cry. Back then I thought she was blaming me for not helping my father. Now I think she was just testing whether I fitted the theory according to which the anorexic is "other-directed," overly dependent on other people's approval and tending to put the interests of others before her own. Who knows. The words are etched in my mind.

Once she asks me to draw her a picture of a place where I would like to live. I start to draw the Smurf land from the comic strip. She asks me if all the Smurfs are boys. I tell her there is one girl in the Smurf village, the Smurf girl. She asks me if I want to be the Smurf girl. I tell her, I do not, because the Smurf girl only causes trouble and conflict. I just want to be a regular Smurf. She looks at me. I blush. She found something. I am caught. I am not normal.

I don't understand. Why don't they cure me? I know they think it has something to do with "gender." My father's alcoholism is behind it. My parents meet with the psychiatrist and the doctor separately. My father refuses to come again. Somehow they blame my mother too; she is upset. Meanwhile they make me go through this labyrinth they have constructed. I am not supposed to know, but they know. They manipulate me, open up some ways, close off others. Drugs, timetables, running, promises, threats. But that is not "treating" me. I wish they would make me feel better. Free me from this prison of my mind! But no, they just create another prison.

I escaped. It is said that behavior modification does not address the root problems of anorexia, but just forces the patients to eat. For this reason it can lead to relapse or even suicide after release from the hospital

(Bruch, 1974). Yes and no. They did question me to find some "causes," but they were looking for causes that proved their predefined hypotheses. They did manipulate me to eat. Although my thoughts continued to revolve around eating for a year after the escape, my weight remained steady. I didn't want to go back to the labyrinth, and I knew how. Stay at 35 kilograms. Little by little I forgot to pay attention to the kilograms.

A nightmare was over. Why was I such a typical "hostile" anorexic patient? After all, weren't they just trying to help me out? Then it starts happening again. While writing the first draft of this book, I go for a short visit to Finland and tell some friends I am writing a book on my anorexia nervosa. They hardly respond; I think they are not interested. After a few days they call my partner in the United States. "Keep an eye on her, she's so skinny and eats so little," they tell him. I am enraged.

I begin to understand my rage. I am enraged about the diagnostic logic, according to which what I say is not to be taken at face value, but is rather to be read as a symptom from which a diagnosis can be made by my psychiatrist, my friends, or any bystander. This omniscience is there in the nurses' handwriting that recorded my every move and saying in the hospital. *She went to the bathroom several times. No signs of vomiting. Today she was feeling sorry for herself and crying. She said she's afraid she will have a nervous breakdown, be put into a mental asylum and never let out.* However, not only health care professionals can occupy the diagnostic position, even if they may have the institutional authority to do so. The diagnostic logic is a cultural and social phenomena, and anyone can try seizing the position of power/knowledge, especially in situations where another individual or group is considered legitimately an object rather than a subject of knowledge (see Foucault, 1978). As a person who has been "disordered," I can easily be rendered the object of diagnosis; not only do my sayings not count, but I am not spoken to. All talk takes place behind my back; even my right to access my medical records can be put to doubt, because of my status as someone unfit to see data collected on her. This story is an attempt to talk back to this diagnostic discourse. Interrupt it.

## *The Mediation*

Anorexia nervosa became a popular topic in the media in the late 1970s and early 1980s, at least in the Western developed countries. The scientific journals and women's magazines were filled with stories explaining the causes and effects of anorexia as well as with descriptions of personal tragedies of celebrities and ordinary schoolgirls. I absorbed them, and so did everyone else; anorexia nervosa was being defined and so was I. I read the stories of anorexics as victims of the thin-body ideal, consumer culture, and affluence; as unwilling to grow up to be a woman; and as neurotic perfectionists formed by overdemanding family environments.

I read the accounts and compared my own experience to them, looking for a match, an explanation, a portrait of myself. It was like reading horoscopes; sometimes I thought the stories highlighted my own self-image, sometimes not. Some of the stories flattered me, others insulted me. In the medical sense my anorexia nervosa ended in perfect recovery. No obsessions about food or body, neither overeating nor dieting. But in another sense this was only the beginning. At school my teachers knew about anorexia and each acted based on their knowledge of it. "You look so good," some of them kept saying. Probably to boost my allegedly poor self-esteem. My math teacher took the liberty of pouring more pork sauce on my plate in the cafeteria.

When the 1970s turned to the 1980s, the media coverage of anorexia intensified. The psychiatric explanations spilled over to women's magazines spiced up with celebrities' stories, such as those of Karen Carpenter and Princess Diana. There were many explanations, but some were more popular in both the scientific and popular media. They solidified into the standard portrait of the anorexic.

By far the most popular narrative is that anorexia nervosa is caused by consumer/beauty culture and the thin-body ideal. This story is embraced by the psychiatric, communications, and feminist scholarship, as well as by the popular media. In my own discipline, communication studies, researchers have designed experimental studies to examine the deleterious effects of media images of thinness. They measure the relationship between exposure to media images of thinness and eating disorders, hypothesizing, for example: "that exposure to thinness-depicting-and-promoting (TDP) media, defined as fitness and fashion magazines and television programs with conspicuously thin female characters, would predict . . . anorexia, bulimia, drive for thinness, body dissatisfaction and ineffectiveness in women" (Harrison, 2000, p. 20). Major and minor celebrities' confessions about anorexia and bulimia saturate the media. One example is Tracy Shaw, who played the hairdresser Maxine in the British soap opera *Coronation Street*. Shaw told the *Sun*, "I was totally obsessed. I used to have dreams about eating fish and chips," and was complimented by a medical commentary: "Dr Moss says: 'It's not surprising that someone like Tracy Shaw ended up with an eating disorder . . . It's definitely related to the lifestyle of a star. Pressure to have good appearance is an important part of life for them'" (Roberts, 2000).

I thought back to my teenage years. I had bad, infected adolescent skin, and I used to be mesmerized by the magnified images of the models' unblemished, velvety skin in glossy teenage magazines. I knew the photographs were airbrushed for any spots or inconsistencies, but I continued to admire and dream of the satiny, smooth cheeks of the women with endless almond eyes in the beauty product spreads. And I kept buying herbal cleansing lotions and thick, beige cover-up creams from mail-order beauty catalogues. So, magazines can aggravate teenage agonies. However, I did not pay much attention to the models' bodies. I had recovered from my anorexia by my teens, but I continued to be pin thin until young adulthood. In my teens I knew I was thinner than any of the models in the magazines, and in that area I did not feel inferior to them. I knew I was too skinny and flat-chested but that did not seem as big of a sin as being too fat, so I was not preoccupied with it.

But was my anorexia precipitated by glossy magazines? As an eleven-year-old working-class Finnish girl, I do not recall having ever held a fashion magazine in my hands, and I am almost certain that Finnish-language fitness magazines did not even exist at that point in time. I try to think back. Did I want to be beautiful and thin? I did not want to be ugly. Fat. All the autobiographies of anorexics are filled with descriptions of how they abhorred fat. I also performed the fat inspection rites like touching my stomach and ribs to make sure there was no fat, and I was obsessed with observing my hairy, peeling, and skinny arms. But it was my own Kafkaesque world—me staring at the hair on my arms. I didn't think of beauty; my thoughts were spinning in circles and stopped at my body hair. But was this after a diet gone wild? I didn't start dieting; as strange as it may sound from our contemporary "obesity epidemic" obsessed perspective, I did not really have an idea of what a "diet" meant. I just stopped eating and drinking. I thought I had some disease. The calorie charts and regular weighing only became part of my routine in the hospital.

"What did fat mean to you then?" somebody asked. I wonder if my culture provides me words to express anything out of the usual. Women are obsessed with their looks/fat. Maybe it had to do with keeping myself together. In my working-class neighborhood the demand was not to be perfect; it was good enough not to let life put you down, to be tough, a survivor. But I had been an exceptionally good student in the local primary school. After third grade my parents, following my pleading and my best friend's parents' example, put me into an expensive, selective private school. The fees were high, but I was the only child and, repeating after the grandmother of my best friend, my mother kept saying: "If you only have one child, you must afford to educate her even to a professor." The first day of my new school I not only entered a more challenging learning environment but also an upper-middle-class world. The expectations were much higher than in my local primary school, and my performance plummeted. I had a hard time at home. I was lonely and sometimes snacked to console myself. I gained some weight, but could not be called fat, and by the time anorexia began my weight was back to usual and I had gotten up from my down. But maybe I associated food with my inability to keep up, which also fits the cultural association between eating and loosing control. And then my mother's friend harassed me with food at that summer cottage, and we visited desolate Lapland. So, these bizarre coincidences and associations made it all break out in relation to eating? I do not know.

I try to think back to a distant and foggy past. I must have wanted to be slender. Why do I not want to fit the narrative of anorexia as an expression of the destructive potential of beauty ideals? Carole Spitzack (1993, pp. 16–18) has pointed out that anorexia represents women as lacking twice. First the anorexics are projected/project themselves as deficient in relation to the beauty ideals. Then they are expected, again, to publicly confess, like Tracy Shaw, their deficiencies as women who fall victims to social ideals and end up obsessed with their body, looks, laxatives, lettuce, fish and chips. I do not want to confess to something of which I am not guilty. I did not starve in a bid to become beautiful, although I was not immune to societal messages that being thin is better than being fat. Furthermore, the idea that anorexics embark on a program of near lethal self-starvation simply because of media images of thinness is hideously stigmatizing and reductionist. It frames women as helplessly, even fatally, vainglorious. It paints a picture of them as weak-minded in the sense of falling victims to fanciful pictures and other vanities of modern consumer culture, selling cheap dreams and creams for social groups with less-critical discerning powers to separate sense from nonsense.

The "scientific" enterprise that measures the level of this folly—by, for example, exposing women to thirty minutes of images of thinness and then calculating their level of body-image distortion (see Myers & Riocca, 1992)—is founded on idiotic reductionism. This reductionism presupposes that one can inject a dosage of culture into people and deliver effects, much the same way as the large, randomized, controlled clinical trials—which I plow through in my current job as a health service researcher—that expose individuals to ninety minutes of lifestyle counseling and measure changed levels of smoking and serum cholesterol four and twelve months after (e.g., Steptoe et al., 1999). Experiments that measure effects or the effectiveness of clinical interventions frequently target vulnerable or deviant groups, such as young women (Myers & Riocca, 1992) or the fat, the smokers, and the ones with high cholesterol (Steptoe et al., 1999). How many times have you heard of a media effects study or a clinical intervention trial targeting middle-class, middle-age, white men? Women have eating disorders in disproportionate numbers and the poor and ethnic minorities have cardiovascular disease and diabetes in disproportionate numbers not because of overexposure or underexposure to media and counseling messages but because of complex, systemic structures of inequality.

Having written the critique, and still feeling the rush of anger through my body, I want to underline that I think critiques of beauty ideals are useful. I think back to the women in the body-image lecture. "Breaking Free" is the title of a series of lectures that take place across North American campuses. I sit at the back and listen to the lecture on the dangers of yo-yo dieting and how we should learn to appreciate different shapes of bodies. The other women seem enthusiastic, burbling in a shy manner, wanting to share their experiences. The critique of narrow and narrow-minded beauty ideals can be empowering, but the fact that this critique remains blind to its reductionist, humiliating, and sexist underside is lamentable. We cannot "break free" from discourses and become our true not-too-thin and not-too-fat selves; rather, we need to become more literate in critically reading the multifaceted politics that discourses urging us to be this or that harbor.

The other canonical story, which is the reverse side of the beauty thesis, is that anorexics do not want to grow up to mature womanhood. Feminists see anorexia as a contradiction; the women are at the same time conforming to the ideal of feminine beauty and rebelling against it (e.g., Bordo, 1993; Mahowald, 1992). It is argued that anorexics rejoice when they stop menstruating due to starving, or they disguise or even self-harm their budding breasts (Mukai, 1988). This anxiety over the female body can be understood as rebellion against limiting gender roles. But it can also aim at suppressing the archetypical negative, voracious, and insatiable notion of femininity (Bordo, 1993).

Contrary to the "typical" anorexic I was not an early maturer. At the onset of my anorexia I had not menstruated, nor had my body begun to take a womanly shape. I don't recall hating the feminine aspects of my body then or later. They told me I would be sterile and would not develop "normally" if I didn't eat. I wasn't thrilled by that, I was concerned. The idea that I could, perhaps, never be a mother worried me.

But then there is me/the Smurf. Back then I thought the psychiatrist was wrong to pick up the boy/girl axis in my story. I liked the Smurf village because of its friendly harmony. The appeal was no conflict, not no girls. But maybe the unconscious came into play. Nevertheless, I ended up identifying myself with a Smurf, even though it remains a mystery if I was a Smurf already before or only after I told the Smurf story. But I found the psychiatrist's look (and the look of many other people to whom I have told the Smurf story) oppressive. I should have wanted to be the Smurf girl. Not wanting to be the Smurf girl was not normal, a psychopathology.

The tenacious Smurf in me has been against being told how to be a woman. Just a few months ago I re-encountered the Smurf discourse, when a colleague of mine commented that I wear clothes that do not show off my body—something she told me is typical of anorexics. At forty I am no longer so enraged or embarrassed by these diagnostic comments. I know the "baggy clothing" theory of anorexia—I know all of them. My colleague likes to wear girlie clothes, such as black spider web hose and high heels, and her favorite theorist is Judith Butler. I muse, with a hint of malice, on what lies behind her need to don out-of-fashion social theories and out-of-fashion attention-getting clothing. I catch myself in the act of retaliating her normative gender slur with normative gender slurs. Whatever a woman wears, whether it is an understated office outfit or provocative black lace and leather, can be interpreted as a symptom of something, such as insecurity or immaturity or a lack of something (approval? originality? confidence? attention?). We have a never-ending opportunity to pass judgment on how each of us does gender, and anorexia is just one in a long line of diagnostic conditions that has defined the parameters of not too understated and not too overstated healthy normal femininity.

The third prototypical characteristic of anorexics is (neurotic) perfectionism. This is reflected in unusually high grades, exaggerated cleanliness and tidiness, and so on. Often the perfectionist narrative is attached to the gender story. It is argued that women are torn between contradictory pressures in contemporary society; today's woman should be a traditional attractive and passive "object" and a modern successful active "subject" at the same time (e.g., Fraad, 1990; Mahowald, 1992).

Hilde Bruch (1978) argues that anorexia is caused by a "paralyzing underlying sense of ineffectiveness" (p. x). The young women feel that they have totally lost control of their lives. This is due to the fact that they have always tried to please others and have never taken their own initiatives. They have eaten the food that has been put on their plate without complaint, they have achieved high grades at school without really considering their goals, or pursued careers that they have not chosen. Anorexia is the final rebellion of these women who have never before caused any trouble. Food intake becomes the sole thing they have absolute control over. Anorexia becomes a struggle for identity and independence.

Bruch's talk about imagining has provoked accusations of downplaying the "real" structures that constrain young women (Gremillion, 1992). Yet, perhaps, the most pervasive feature of Bruch's and her many followers' analysis is the stress on the "neurotic" character of all anorexics' activity. Bruch goes so far as to refute the girls' intelligence. Bruch notes that they are actually stuck in an earlier nondifferentiated developmental stage and are incapable of conceptual and independent evaluation. Bruch states that

> anorexics usually excel in their school performance, and this has been interpreted as indicating high intelligence and giftedness; the discovery that we now have made of real defects in conceptualization was unexpected. The excellent academic achievements are not uncommonly the results of great effort. Sometimes it comes as a shock that performance on college aptitude tests, or other examinations of ability, falls below what had been expected on the basis of excellent school grades. (Bruch, 1978, p. 48)

Thus Bruch distinguishes between the real intelligence (as shown in the aptitude tests) and forced intelligence (which is the sign of the anorectic neurosis).

In my hospital records there is a short note: *School performance: Spring semester has gone well. Has received special tutoring in mathematics. Math grade: B.* The judgment is clear: my perfectionism, or my parents' perfectionism, is demonstrated by the fact that I have received special tutoring in a situation where my performance is good (the note does not tell that when I began receiving special tutoring I had received a D in math—unheard of in my high-ability school).

Thirteen years after I escaped from the hospital I dare to go to see a psychologist for the first time. I am planning my master's thesis. I sit in the chair and start talking.

> "My problem is that I always set myself really high goals."
> "You attain them?"
> "Yes."
> "Maybe you shouldn't then think of that as your problem but as your strength."
> A chain broke.

When I had anorexia I was not a good pupil. Coming from an uneducated family and a primary school that demanded little, I could not initially meet the expectations in my new upper-middle-class school. But all the high grades, praises, awards, and scholarships that came afterwards always carried a bitter undertone with them. Maybe I was trying neurotically hard. But I loved studying; my father, who thought that healthy children spent their time playing outside, used to hide my books so I would not waste my time "rotting" inside the house.

Meritocracy. My cousins from Lapland, my childhood friends, and my other relatives have all disappeared from my life. I am an academic who has lived in many countries, and made a career and a comfortable even if continuously precarious living out of it. My young son follows in his mother's footsteps and goes to a selective private school. Being a lively male child, his teachers comment that his behavior could be improved but compliment him for his academic achievements, which they attribute to him being very clever. I think back to Walkerdine's (1993) discussion on how educational and developmental psychology is founded upon a sexist and classist normative notion of a naturally naughty, playful, and creative male child—Rousseau's Emile. I think how this romance with the free-spirited male child frames my son's academic success as a sign of high intelligence and how it framed my academic success as a sign of neurotic fastidiousness. It might be reasonable to critically reflect on my current privilege in terms of socioeconomic and symbolic capital. Yet, I/the gendered discourse on intelligence and education should not deprive me of pride with my work because anorexic (female) success is not a sign of a genuine talent but just disingenuine or strained hard work.

## *My Story*

Every anorexic has her story, one that's often articulated amidst the gallery of anorexic stereotypes that abound in the scientific literature, the caretaking realm, in the media, and in everyday life. My struggle with the discourses on anorexia became my still-continuing story. But I have my favorite story, too. Maybe anorexics need an explanation in order to recover—a healing story. Maybe not. A story to satisfy our vigorous craving for final explanations.

My favorite story has, not surprisingly, to do with the family. There is extensive literature on the dysfunctions of anorexics' families. One of the first and, perhaps, most influential accounts of the family problems behind anorexia again is Hilde Bruch's. Bruch paints a portrait of her patients' typical family (Bruch, 1978). The prototype mother of an anorexic daughter is dominant, almost tyrannical, and has gotten overinvolved in her daughter's life. The mother dictates the young woman's life, overprotects her, and projects her hopes on her. The boundary between the two individuals dissolve. Enmeshment ensues. The father is in the background, typically less involved in family affairs. Perhaps he is busy pursuing a career.

This daughter is somehow special for the family. Since her very birth she has been paid extra attention, and she has filled the dreams and expectations of the parents so far. The family is usually affluent. The daughter has received everything she has ever wanted and feels she doesn't deserve it. She becomes the sparrow in the golden cage.

Bruch's arguments have been widely appropriated. Yet she has also been criticized for ignoring the role of the father (Horsfall, 1991). The dominant-mother and weak-father dyad has been challenged in many studies. Alternative prototypes have been suggested, while other studies have not found any prototypes.

My/my psychiatrist's/my mother's story about my anorexia has never focused on my mother. My father has always been the central figure. He was an alcoholic. My clearest childhood memories are of laying on my bed, listening to the sound of the elevator and being afraid it would stop at our floor and my father would come home drunk. At times he would wake me up and tell me about his unhappy childhood. He was in a foster home, on a farm. He was the youngest son there. They cared for him. His mother came and took him back when he was six. Later she put him in an orphanage. Once my father asked me what I would do if he committed suicide by leaping from our balcony. He made gestures that suggested going to the balcony. We lived on the sixth floor. I cried and begged him not to do it.

I was sitting on a tram. I carried a cheap red plastic travel bag. I had my nightgown and toiletries in there. I was on my way to my aunt's. My mother was working (she was a waitress and often worked night shifts), and I did not want to be at home when my father came home drunk. I also spent nights at my other aunt's. Overprotective home? Dependent child? The year before I was hospitalized because of the stomachaches, a nurse once asked me if I wanted to stay at the hospital. "No," I said. I lied. I didn't want to go home.

Two years after I had escaped from the hospital, my father got a temporary job at a Finnish construction project in the then–Soviet Union. While he was there, my mother decided to divorce him. Or rather I did. I shouted at my mother that she had to decide if it was me or him that would go. Had I not almost lost my mind because of him? Maybe I made that sentence up later. Nevertheless, I felt I caused my mother's and my father's divorce. But I never felt submissive or obedient. I was in command. Since everyone else in the house was out of control, I had to be in control. I was the one who applied to a good, private school, got out of the hospital, got the divorce. . . . My parents merely had to sign the documents and the occasional check. And most of the time I felt I was on top of things, though occasionally I felt I could not keep up.

After the divorce I did not see my father for almost a year. Then we met in a cafe. He had lost weight and he looked older. He had lived that winter in the homeless shelters. But now he had moved in with a woman he had met in a restaurant. Once I went to a pub with my father. He told me that he wanted to move out of the woman's place because he did not love her. He told me he would like to go work on an oil rig in Norway and earn good money. He would then be able to buy a two-bedroom apartment, where the two of us could live. I tried to explain him that it was not so much a question of love, but that he had a place to live and someone who cared for him. I didn't want to take care of him. The last thing I wanted was to share a flat with him.

Soon after we learned that my father had lung cancer. Decades of working underground amidst rock dust as a drill operator and smoking a pack of cigarettes a day. First he was fine. But then suddenly they called me from the hospital and told that he had almost died the night before. He was in great pain and thirsty. He was running a high temperature, was too weak to drink by himself, and had to be given fluids with a beaker. He wanted me to give him Donald Duck pear lemonade, a children's favorite. I lifted the beaker, full of bright green, fizzy liquid, to his dry, chapped, and pale lips every half an hour. I had a summer job as a journalist at a provincial newspaper three hours away from the hospital in Helsinki. I traveled back and forth between there and Helsinki, sleeping at the back of the bus. On my father's fifty-fifth birthday, I arrived at the hospital at eleven at night. I spent the night with him, half asleep on a stretcher. My father kept coughing and asking for a drink. The next morning his partner came to change shifts with me. My father asked me to stay for another night. I had a day off the day after, but I wanted to go to Tampere, where I studied, and stay the night at my boyfriend's place. I needed consoling. I kissed my father good-bye and told him I loved him. He refused to answer. He died that night. I later realized he knew he would.

Years later I participated in a course on psychodrama just for fun. I acted out a scene from my childhood where my father was drunk and sobbing. All the anger, the love, and the helplessness poured out. The leader of the course said to me that maybe I should try to distinguish between the drunkard, who made his child's life hell, and the other father, whom I loved. A picture from our family album surges into my mind. I am looking into my father's eyes. My round face lifted up, eyes beaming, my thick hair disobediently dissolving my brown braids. I laugh. My father looks down upon me, smiling.

Last night I was trying to think about a story that would convey that father. I tried several times, but couldn't find a good scene. Where are my words? I stare at the computer screen. I burst into tears. Where is the little round-faced girl? Speak. Tell what is in those eyes. I have no words.

He is only in the tears. Did my anorexia story bury this story? Probably. Forgiving—myself and him. It was necessary not to let his desperation and yearning for love drain my spirit. It was not necessary to create a one-dimensional story about the guilty parents. Experience is not linear, with a simple cause and an effect, a beginning and an end. It is rather a knot in a messy web; it is connected to a complexity of practices, histories, social structures, pure chances, and discourses that elude complete final mapping. During the years, little by little, my favorite story has fallen apart—the story about my anorexia and the Tyrannical Father, a variation of the canonical Tyrannical Mother.

So how do we connect this family tragedy to the larger social context? It is entangled in many threads. The gender axis. But our story has one axis that I consider especially important: class. We didn't come from Hilde Bruch's young, rich, and beautiful patients' suburbia. We lived in a dark one-bedroom apartment on the east side of Helsinki. My father and my mother drifted south from the poorest northern and eastern provinces of Lapland and Carelia to look for a living. Our history included landless poor, wars, slaughter, misguided revolutions. Broken dreams. Broken people. Executed men. Abused women. Abandoned children. My father/me didn't have a happy childhood. How many generations back? Me trying to deal with my father, my mother, and with my too-difficult school. My father trying to deal with his memories, the booze, the hard labor, the periodic unemployment. My mother working as a waitress during the nights. Suicides. Early deaths. Children not recognized or cared for. Anorexia.

When anorexic, I attributed my starving partly to pure coincidence and to the chaos at home and to my difficulties at school. I found the theories on beauty ideals and perfectionism alienating and insulting. With hindsight I have begun to see my anorexia slightly differently. Theorists who have read anorexia through the meanings associated with the body have been too fixated on gender and forgetful of the way in which the body is a potent symbol that can communicate many social desires and inequalities (but see Thompson, 1994). I have begun to view my anorexia as an attempt to surpass the unruliness of my working-class home, which I frequently compared with my new school friends' middle-class, spacious homes, their diets of yogurt and fresh fruit, their comfortable lives, eloquent parents, and what I thought were much happier and safer families. Partly my commitment to stop eating may have had to do with an oblique attempt to attain a middle-class, composed, and controlled disposition, which draws attention to the way in which inequalities do not only have to do with differences in economic and symbolic capital, but also embodied capital, which underlines the stability of these multiply embedded structures of power.

My explanation of my anorexia, thirty years after the event, as a rather violent attempt to negotiate my personal life and social position is not, of course, divorced from the discourses on anorexia and embodiment, even if it draws attention to slightly different themes. However, it is the explanation that I feel most comfortable with at this moment.

## *Conclusion*

My attempt in this chapter has been to provide an experience-close reflection on the way in which diagnostic and popular public discourses define anorexic women. I have constructed what could loosely be termed a "layered account" (Ronai, 1998), meaning that I have layered discourses that diagnose anorexia and my own experience of being the object of those discourses. The aim of such layered accounts is to set the discourses interrogated into motion.

Clinical, popular, and even feminist discourses on anorexia seem to "help" anorexics by enabling them to regain weight and health and addressing the underlying psychological and familial issues, harmful discourses, and gendered inequalities. The trouble with this "helping" is that it masks the sheer violence and disrespect embedded in the way in which anorexics are treated in psychiatric environments. It also obfuscates the sexist and reductionist underpinnings of discourses that analyze the social ramifications of eating disorders. The clinical explanations and treatments have proceeded largely undebated, even if anorexia is admitted to be unusually hard to treat with high relapse and mortality rates (e.g., Herzog et al., 1999; Millar et al., 2005). Anorexics' critique of the way in which they are treated "for their own good" has been ignored as women with eating disorders are considered notoriously stubborn and defiant, and their resistance to treatment has been swiftly attributed to their sheer irrationality, such as "psychotic development" in my case. Similarly, accusations that analyses of beauty ideals frame women as dupes (Davis, 1995) have been met with counterarguments that discourses operate behind our backs (Bordo, 1997), which basically reinstates the idea that women with eating disorders operate under false consciousness.

I am sure that many health care professionals genuinely try to help anorexic women to recover and that thin beauty ideals are harmful. My introspective analysis has aimed to interrogate, from the inside out, the security in which clinical sciences and social commentators have gone about their business of diagnosing psychological and social ills manifesting themselves in the anorexic woman. It has been my aim to demonstrate that these discourses have rarely addressed their harmful and violent underside. It has also been my aim to fight back against the tendency to silence anorexic women's criticism of their treatment and the way in which they are described in public media, and to underline the need to listen to anorexic women's views of the discourses and practices that are allegedly helping them.

The second goal of this chapter is to experiment with the autobiographic form in an attempt to find a way of communicating about eating disorders that does not simply validate diagnostic notions. Autobiographies by anorexics are not rare; they almost form a popular genre of their own. The first autobiographies on anorexia in the 1970s were written by celebrities, such as Cherry Boone-O'Neill's (Pat Boone's daughter) 1982 *Starving for Attention*, and Kelsey Kirkland's 1987 *Dancing on My Grave*. Examples of more recent and more self-consciously autobiographic accounts are Stephanie Grant's 1996 *Passion of Alice* and Catherine Garrett's 1999 partly autobiographic *Beyond Anorexia: Narrative, Spirituality and Recovery*. While I have enjoyed reading these very different autobiographical accounts, I have found it troubling that they all take anorexia for granted. Boone-O'Neill interprets her anorexia as an expression of her need for attention and approval in a famous family, whereas Garrett associates both her descent into anorexia and recovery from it with a spiritual quest. While I grant that anorexia may in many cases be related to seeking acceptance and that healing can become a quest for reconnecting with nature and the spiritual, I find it problematic that Boone-O'Neill and Garrett bypass the fact that understanding and acting on anorexia in these specific ways articulate predominant trends in psychological theory and practice in the early 1980s and late 1990s respectively. By presenting these psychological interpretations as if coming from the heart they lend them existential and emotional credibility, which makes it difficult to interrogate their social commitments or to entertain other ways of thinking about and acting upon anorexia.

Following the lead of authors who have written autobiographies informed by poststructuralism (Bordowitz, 1994; Minh Ha, 1989; Ronai, 1998), I have in this chapter applied and further developed such a critically self-reflective autoethnography. Discussing the interest in postcolonial studies to allow "the Real Other to speak the 'truth' on otherness," Trinh Minh-Ha (1989) warns of the temptation to succumb to the offered role of the victim, which runs the danger of perpetuating the dominant discourses that have designated the speaking position. Reflecting on the opportunities for Other women to speak, Minh-Ha states:

> Thus, in designating herself as one of the designated others (a form of self-location and self-criticism within established bound-

aries), it is also necessary that she actively maintains the dialectical relation between acceptance and refusal, between reversing and displacing that makes possible the ceaseless questioning of this regime. (Minh-Ha, 1986)

Trinh Minh-Ha highlights the difficulty in speaking one's heart in a situation where the speaking position is saturated with reified expectations. This saturation makes it easy to slip into saying what everyone wants to hear. In autobiographies on anorexia, this often seems to entail confessing being a victim of prevailing notions of beauty and success. While I would grant that thin-body ideals may inform individual women's starving, narratives on body ideals easily become repetitive, making it impossible to address other issues or to problematize the weary assumptions accompanying these self-stories. I have in this chapter tried to voice certain concerns as someone who has experienced anorexia and, at the same time, problematize the expectations audiences usually have of the anorexic voice. Following Minh-Ha, my attempt has been to both accept and refuse the speaking position of the anorexic and to redirect the conversation to slightly different tracks.

# 3

## *Fat Boys and Goody Girls*
### Hilde Bruch's Work on Eating Disorders and the American Ideal of Freedom

There are a few classical historical works in which the emergence of anorexia as a clinical category in the nineteenth century has been investigated (Brumberg, 1988; also Hepworth, 1999). In this chapter I will examine a later period, when the notion of the anorexic as an overly good middle-class girl victimized by parental and media pressures to be dutiful and thin—the notion which informed my own treatment—became consolidated.

To get a feel for the literature in the area, I first conducted an informal survey of the medical literature on the condition from the early twentieth century onwards. This exercise taught me three things. First, the range of material was too large for it to be meaningfully analyzed. Second, the literature revealed that a wealth of biomedical and psychological schools of thought had been employed to explain and treat eating disorders, ranging from genetics and endocrinology to behaviorism, psychoanalysis, and art therapy. Third, the American psychiatrist Hilde Bruch's research on eating disorders came into relief as the most influential work in terms of defining

---

This chapter originally appeared as "Fat Boys and Goody Girls" in *Weighty Issues: The Construction of Fatness and Thinness as Social Problems*, J. Sobal and D. Maurer (eds.), copyright © 1999 by Aldine Publishers. Reprinted by permission of Aldine Transaction, a division of Transaction Publishers. The original was extensively revised for this book.

the medical and popular terms we use to make sense of eating disorders. Because of Bruch's central role in defining the central dogma of anorexia I will explore her work in the historical context in detail.

Bruch was part of the group of psychiatrists who designed the first definition of anorexia nervosa for the third edition of the American Psychiatric Association's *Diagnostic and Statistical Manual of Mental Disorders* (DSM III) in 1980 (APA, 1980). Her popular book on anorexia, *The Golden Cage: The Enigma of Anorexia Nervosa*, published in 1978, shaped the popular understanding of anorexia; when it was reissued by Harvard University Press in 2001 it had sold 150,000 copies, which is a remarkable achievement for a psychology book. Her clippings archive demonstrates that Bruch not only published in major psychiatric journals but also frequently presented her work in the media, from talk shows to magazines such as *Ladies' Home Journal*. Bruch's path-breaking research and her ability to disseminate her views through official and popular channels account for the fact that her definition of anorexia still forms the foundation of our understanding of the condition. Furthermore, what makes Bruch's work particularly interesting to study is that she conducted research both on obesity and anorexia, thereby highlighting the connections between the definitions of the two eating disorders. Bruch's long career, which spanned from the thirties to the seventies, also provides a good opportunity to examine how changing historical conditions have shaped the way eating too little or too much is understood.

To examine the historical context of Bruch's work, I will locate it within developments in world history, in the history of psychiatry, and in her personal biography. I will analyze Bruch's work against the backdrop of U.S. history from post-Depression time to the Cold War period. I will also situate her writing within the shifting trends in psychiatry from the thirties, when the field was still marked by hereditary and eugenic theories of mental illness with their racist undertones, until the postwar psychoanalytic boom. I will also discuss how Bruch's personal history as a German Jewish exile and her personal and professional connections and contexts shaped her perceptions of her patients. This historical analysis is based on Bruch's published works as well as on her reference material, correspondence, and patient files archived in the Texas Medical Center Library.[1]

My historical analysis of Bruch's work is, to use Foucault's (1984b) term, "genealogical" (also Dean, 1994). A common form of conducting historical research into illnesses or social problems is to examine their origins in particular social circumstances. For example, researchers have investigated how anorexia has its roots in the emergence of a separate period of adolescence within a particular middle-class culture and with the increasing prominence of mass media, which propagated the ideal of female thinness (Brumberg, 1988). Historical analysis searching for origins of a phenomenon asks: Why did obesity or anorexia begin to increase in a particular historical moment? Genealogy, on the other hand, troubles the category of anorexia that the other approach seeking origins takes for granted. It asks: Why and how did we begin to think of obesity and anorexia as diseases in a particular historical moment? As the goal of my book is to interrogate discourses on anorexia, a genealogical approach to historiography is fitting.

The key project of this chapter is to explore the connection between Hilde Bruch's theories on obesity and anorexia. Bruch defines both the obese and the anorexics in largely the same terms. Both are seen as suffering from an insufficiently autonomous ego precipitated by a suffocating family environment. The similarity of the theories is all the more surprising as Bruch conducted her research on obesity and anorexia in significantly different contexts. Her research on the endocrinological roots of obesity in a large public hospital in the post-Depression New York City in the 1930s focused on poor immigrant children. Her study included both boys and girls, but it famously refuted the so-called Froehlich's syndrome, a supposed endocrinological malfunction that was alleged to cause obesity and genital malformation in boys (Bruch, 1939a). Bruch concluded that there was nothing wrong with the boys' metabolism; they simply ate too much because of their mothers' dysfunctional and authoritarian relationship with them, which was already present in the way in which they fed the boys as infants. Bruch's research on anorexia happened in a rather different environment. In the 1950s she had set up a private psychoanalytic practice and her anorexic clientele was mainly upper middle class. Still, Bruch concluded that the problem with the anorexic girls could also be traced to mothering. Their overpowering mothers were alleged to have raised them to be too good, obsessively trying to be thin and beautiful and dutiful in their schoolwork.

My contention is that regardless of the different historical circumstances, Bruch's work on both obesity and anorexia was guided by a similar anxiety about personal freedom, which strongly resonated with the political culture and situation of the times. The fat immigrant boys Bruch studied in the post-Depression era became symbols of the traditional or authoritarian habits of their foreign families, and fit the general social mood, which perceived new immigrants as a threat to American values and democracy. The too-good, middle-class anorexic girls, whom Bruch treated later, became symbols of their middle-class families' socially conformist values and lifestyle, which resonated with the postwar concern with the new suburban middle class and its mass culture, associated with fascism and communism.

The similarities between Bruch's theories on obesity and anorexia help us to understand the emergence of the paradox that the anorexic, who starves to escape the negative characteristics associated with fatness, such as lack of mental strength and independence, will be defined as lacking the very same qualities of mental and physical fitness (see Gremillion, 2003).

My analysis of Bruch's work has two main goals. First, by exploring the historical contingency of her theories on eating disorders I hope to destabilize them as timeless truths about what is wrong with individuals who are perceived to be too fat or thin. By doing that I will hopefully loosen the normative grip of the ideal of mental strength and fitness that drives anorexics to starve and then, paradoxically and counterproductively, informs their treatment. Second, I want to explore the complex and contradictory politics articulated by Bruch's theories on obesity and anorexia. Bruch did not explain the immigrant children's obesity as a result of their metabolism and genes but argued that the problem was their culture. Her theory challenged often eugenic ways of explaining health and social problems but also launched a double-edged therapeutic effort to change obese immigrant children's families' culture or attitudes. Bruch's theory on anorexia criticized the 1950s suburban life and its domesticated femininity, but its idealization of strength and autonomy also blindly embraced a rugged, masculine American individualism with all its psychological and political contradictions. My aim in this chapter is to unpack the history of the multidimensional threads intertwined in the diagnostic discourse on anorexia in order to better understand their psychologically and politically both empowering and disempowering dimensions.

## *Early Theories of Obesity: Weak Morals, Races, and Metabolism*

Hilde Burch was born in 1905 in Dülken to a middle-class German Jewish family. She had recently received a degree in pediatric medicine when she fled from the intensifying anti-Semitism, first to England in 1933, and then to the United States in 1934 (Hatch-Bruch, 1996).

Bruch began her work on eating disorders soon after she arrived to the United States in the mid thirties. She was working at the Babies' Hospital in New York City, where she was asked to establish an endocrine clinic for fat children. By the thirties, obesity was firmly established as a medical and aesthetic problem (Schwarz, 1986; Stearns, 1997). The idea of an endocrine clinic stemmed from the assumption that fatness was caused by slow metabolism. Other influential theories of obesity of the time—against and through which Bruch defined her ideas—traced it to, for example, the person's hereditary physical and mental constitution or lack of moral strength.

The early-twentieth-century hereditary theory of obesity was closely linked to the contemporary speculations about the connections between body shape, personality, and intellectual endowment (e.g., Sheldon, 1940, 1942). These theories articulated often racist ideas about how certain body structures corresponded with intelligence levels or particular behaviors, such as insanity or criminality. The most devastating outcome of these eugenistic ideas was the Nazi Holocaust. In the United States, speculation about body shape and character was often related to the anxiety caused by new immigrants from Southern and Eastern Europe, who were feared to be bringing bad genes to the American stock. The genetic theories on the link between a specific body shape and intelligence and behavior formed part of the basis for the government's policy to start screening the physical appearance and intelligence of immigrants at the border and later to establish stricter immigration laws (Jimenez, 1993; Kraut, 1994).

Not surprisingly, then, scientific and popular discussions on obesity focused on whether it was more prevalent among specific ethnic and religious groups, and it was noted that blacks, Jews, and Roman Catholics were more likely to be fat than white Protestants (Preble, 1915). This observation was sometimes articulated into theories that aimed to establish a relationship between a "lower" race and obesity. Angel (1949), for example, was surprised to find that the obese women in his large survey came from established American families. Angel speculated that their body shape and the higher-than-average frequency of Catholic backgrounds indicated that they represented the "alpine" and other "rugged" stocks of Europeans:

> The sample's ancestries stress the parts of Europe where Alpine (and other more rugged) "survivors" of Upper Paleolithic European populations are relatively numerous . . . . Thus the type distribution . . . classifies over half of the series as showing phenotypic trait combinations which are thought to have been evolved in Europe during the last glacial period. Less than one fifth of the series approximates the long-headed types characteristic of various people who penetrated Europe from southeast to northwest during the great population expansion of the third millennium B.C. and who revolutionized the ecology of the area by bringing first farming and later urban civilization from the Near East. (Angel, 1949, p. 442)

Thus, Angel mixed theories on prehistoric migration, ethnicity, and body shape to perform a complex task of connecting a robust or "rugged" body shape, ethnic and religious origin, and cultural or civilizational inferiority. In this mélange the obese were established as representing the surviving members of a stocky Alpine race developed in Europe during the last Ice Age, as opposed to "long-headed" civilized populations, who came to the continent later and brought with them both agriculture and urban habitation.

The moral theory of obesity, which enjoyed popularity at the same time as the biological one, defined obesity as a simple sign of gluttony. The moral theory often associated overeating with the new consumer culture and invasive femininity of shopping women (see Stearns, 1997). The moral theory condemned obesity both as a personal character flaw and as socially irresponsible; for example, large people were framed as "parasites" amidst the Depression-era scarcity (Chang & Christakis, 2002). Moralizing tones were often evident in depictions of fat people as jolly, round hedonists devouring rich foods. An illuminating although quite late example of this theory is an ad from the early fifties for the diet pill Dexedrin.[2] It has two pictures: one of a large happily smiling woman eating cake and surrounded by rich desserts, and another one of a slim, sullen woman surrounded by a pile of dirty dishes, a cleaning bucket, and a baby. The ad states Dexedrin works both as an appetite suppressant (referring to the fat woman) and as an antidepressant (referring to the overworked homemaker).

The ad also illuminates the historicity of theories of obesity. The image of a widely smiling fat woman amidst desserts seems foreign to a contemporary reader, because we are accustomed to psychological theories on obesity and bouts of overeating marked by depression and self-loathing. The juxtaposition of a happy fat woman and an unhappy thin one does not simply make immediate sense.

Bruch originally followed the endocrinological theory of obesity, which understood obesity to be caused by a slow metabolism. It was thought that metabolism could be accelerated by the then-popular glandular injections. Endocrinologists often diagnosed young chubby boys with Froehlich's syndrome, a supposed pituitary dysfunction understood to cause obesity, genital underdevelopment, and overall effeminate and infantile appearance. However, different theories were often intermeshed. Endocrinology was, for instance, mixed with constitutional theories to support racist and other myths. An example of this is Garrison's (1922) speculation about the metabolic origin of the "generic sexuality" of "negroes" or the characteristic "frigidity" or "flabbiness" of the obese (pp. 70–71).

So, Bruch initiated her study of a hundred obese 2 to 13 year-old children in her new endocrine clinic.[3] Half of them were boys and half of them were girls. As the hospital was located in New York City and was a product of the Progressive Era's public health movement against infant mortality, the children came from relatively poor families. The theories making connections between race and obesity were of particular importance as most of the children were of East European Jewish, and to a lesser extent Italian and Irish, immigrant origin (Bruch, 1939a, 1957, pp. 112–115).

Bruch set out to measure the metabolism of the children, but her case notes[4] also reflect the influence of constitutional notions of obesity. Bruch carefully noted down the nationality and religion of the children's parents. Besides measuring height and weight, she also made notes of the form of the children's skulls, their eyes, face, hair, genitals, and general appearance. In some cases, Bruch recorded peculiar features, such as "heavy jaw" or "coarse hair," associated with the different constitutional/racial/endocrinological types, but she paid closest attention to the distribution of fat within the body, as glandular disorders were understood to cause the accumulation of fat in extraordinary places. Both IQ and the Rorschach inkblot tests were used to measure any abnormalities in the children's intelligence and personality.

Although Bruch never denied the impact of heredity or metabolism on obesity, her early studies concluded that their role was overemphasized and misguiding. In a series of famous articles, she refuted Froehlich's syndrome and associated theories, arguing that the children's physical or genital development was not retarded (Bruch, 1939a). She also argued that the children's metabolism was normal; they simply ate too large quantities of food and were unusually inactive (Bruch, 1939b). On the contrary, Bruch indicated that there seemed to be "something wrong" with the children's interaction with their mothers, which became evident during the consultation:

> It was noted that with great frequency even older children (10 years or more) were unable to dress and undress themselves and accepted help from their parents in a matter-of-fact way, as if they were accustomed to being waited on. A similar attitude was sometimes expressed as soon as the patient and his mother entered the examination room. The room is equipped with one chair beside the desk of the physician, which is usually taken by the mother. Obese children often took the chair while the mother stood and remained seated, with the mother's approval, even when it was suggested that the chair be offered to the mother. (Bruch, 1939a, p. 1088)

Bruch's hypothesis that "the degree of self care and independence" of the children was seriously hampered directed her attention to the immigrant women's mothering (Bruch, 1939a, p. 1089).

## Neurotic Mothers and Claustrophobic Immigrant Quarters

After her initial studies in the thirties, Bruch became one of the pioneers who turned attention away from physical theories of obesity, which sometimes contained racist undertones, and toward theories focusing on family interaction and lifestyle. It could be said that as a Jew who had fled the Nazi Holocaust, it would have been difficult for Bruch to explain the obesity of Jewish children by their biological constitution. Personal issues aside, Bruch's work also belongs to the wartime trend in American psychiatry away from hereditary and racial theories toward hygienic explanations that stressed the importance of environmental factors in producing social, mental, or physical deviance. This new trend criticized the harsh measures of deportation and sterilization, which were often supported by eugenistically oriented scholarship and which were implemented to deal with the deviance these theories presented as genetically, and thus incurably, flawed. Instead the new scholars believed in the powers of education and therapy, and in this they continued the earlier legacy of asylum and charity activism (e.g., Grob, 1984).

In her exploration of the family constellation of the obese children, Bruch noted that the families were poor.[5] They lived in small and crowded apartments, often with grandparents. Bruch considered that this explained the unusual inactivity of the children as there was little room to play. Bruch also remarked that the families spent a disproportionate amount of their money on food and did not provide their children adequate clothing or "tools and equipment for play and athletics" (Bruch & Touraine, 1940, p. 153). Describing the parents, Bruch noted that the fathers were weak, lacking in ambition and initiative and unable to provide for the family (pp. 154–155). Bruch's main focus was on the mothers, though. She observed that they had fewer children than the average, had often had several abortions, and had not wanted the obese child. In the notebooks Bruch made most notes on the mothers' "nervous system." The women were described, for example, as "quiet," "upset," "unstable and impulsive," or "talkative and excitable." In the published text, they were described as "self-pitying women" who had been frustrated in their dreams of a "life of ease and luxury" (p. 158) in the United States and who projected their own bitterness and insecurity on the children. These women beat their children, and yet they overprotected them and stuffed them with food to pacify them and to assuage their own guilt. The resulting children were clinging and flaccid, and they ate enormously. Bruch's stern and patronizing stance toward the immigrant families is highlighted, for instance, in the following:

> The [child's] father is [himself] the youngest of five children. "He is the unsuccessful one of my children," says his mother, who resents the presence of his family in her overcrowded apartment. The mother . . . avoids discussion of her early life except to recount her adolescent popularity. "I never bothered with my family, I was the one having a good time." But at 42 years she displays a strong tie to her mother, which supersedes all other personal relationships. She is an immature and unreliable person who covers up real issues and facts in her life, and refuses to face realities, just as she blondines her hair and covers her wrinkles with gaudy make-up. (p. 158)

The previous quote and Bruch's work as a whole manifest that, although she stressed the importance of the environment in causing obesity, her understanding of it was fairly narrow. Even as Bruch observed the families' arduous living conditions, she focused her attention on the mothers' attitudes and comportment and father's lack of entrepreneurship. For instance, instead of relating the mothers' frequent abortions and reluctance to have children to the lack of contraceptive choices and to the difficulties of bringing up children under conditions of poverty, Bruch observes these facts in terms of the psychological damage done to the "unwanted" obese child. These analyses and Bruch's judgmental remarks about the frivolity of the immigrants—manifested in her comments about their lack of industriousness, dreams of ease and luxury, and even their use of cosmetics—focus on the families' lifestyle and attitudes. Thus, even if Bruch observed the social and economic hardships facing the immigrants in post-Depression New York City, she turned her attention to their comportment and stamina.

Despite these moralizing tones, Bruch did not per se underwrite the moral explanation of obesity. On the contrary, she criticized the physicians and the general public for treating the fat with "unmitigated scorn," which she argued only makes them more miserable (Bruch, 1957, pp. 36–38). The therapeutic approach, which Bruch represented, did not view the obese as primarily culpable for their condition but more as its victims (Chang & Christakis, 2002). This approach underlined fat people's limited ability to perceive and pursue other modes of living. Because of their limited capacities, the obese were diagnosed as in need of expert medical and therapeutic advice, provided by professionals like Bruch. The therapeutic rhetoric and practice was more humane than the genetic or moralizing explanations of obesity, as it set out more explicitly to "help" the obese to lead a healthier life. This helping sometimes took the form of public service provision to improve the lot of the disenfranchised in terms of education, health care, and so on, but it also provided new opportunities for the expanding private health care, market. Yet, the therapeutic stance also echoed the moralistic stance, as it still underlined the individual's responsibility in losing weight or, in the case of the obese child, the family's responsibility in making the child lose weight, even if the people were seen to need outside help to do this. Furthermore, all the theories on obesity, including the therapeutic, moralistic and endocrinological theories, shared the aim of measuring people against a generalized norm. Children's body weight was one of these norms. Its monitoring gained unprecedented momentum with new tools, such as weight charts, made possible by the increasing use of statistical methods that yielded data on "the normal" based on large populations (e.g., Miller & O'Leary, 1994; Polsky, 1991).

Bruch's psychological theory of obesity belongs to the larger body of works that marked a watershed in professions dealing with deviance of different sorts. Perspectives were changing away from fatalistic hereditary and harshly judgmental moral perspectives toward new therapeutic or neo-hygienist approaches. These new approaches did not locate the origin of obesity or criminality in the people's genes but in their behaviors and culture. The project then became not necessarily to exclude or eliminate these groups from the "normal" population but to change their habits and cultures. The idea that a certain trait or behavior, such as a large body, is a problem of culture attaches it to a broad normative agenda for everyday life. For example, for Bruch the problem was not merely the children's body weight. Her comments on the immigrant families' home and family size, their consumption patterns, their manners, their use of cosmetics, and their ways of raising children entangle body weight with issues belonging to multiple spheres of life. All in all, Bruch's agenda interpreted the immigrant families' problems as resulting from their inability to live up to the white middle-class family ideal, which reached its apex in the fifties. This ideal demanded "a carefree, child-centered outlook—with relaxed methods of child discipline, separate rooms for each child, and educational toys and music lessons" (Mintz & Kellogg, 1988, p. 187).

To conclude, Bruch's research on obesity rejected the racist and violent agenda of the eugenists that had exerted a considerable influence in the field in the early twentieth century. However, even if it did not define the immigrant families' genes as the problem, it continued to consider these groups as a potential threat to the American social and moral order, even if the threat was now posed by their authoritarian lifestyle rather than their inferior DNA. Furthermore, Bruch's critique of authoritarianism not only reflected the national anxiety about immigrants, but also resonated with international sensibilities at a moment when the United States was entering the war against the continental powers, fomenting a nationalist sentiment in defense of its "free" political and social system. The critique of authoritarianism was also consonant with American psychiatry's turning toward Freudianism and its anti-repressive agenda, as well as Bruch's own traumatic experiences as a Jew in the Germany of the 1930s. Thus Bruch's theory of obesity was intermeshed with international, national, psychiatric, and personal historical agendas of the time; it projected them onto the immigrant children, who became symbols of the authoritarianism, and the adherence to tradition, associated with their poor, foreign-born families. In short, the fat children became the antithesis for notions of individual freedom and democracy, strongly associated with America at the time.

## The Authoritarian Personality and Infant Feeding

During the Second World War, Bruch pursued her interest in family dynamics by specializing in psychiatry and underwent psychoanalysis with fellow German Jewish exile Frieda Fromm-Reichmann. Bruch soon established herself as an expert in child psychiatry and eating problems, and her clientele began to include more middle-class private patients. The patients were at first mostly young obese women, and later young anorexic women. Bruch's turn to psychoanalysis parallels a general interest in Freud in American psychiatry after the war. Both the First and the Second World Wars increased interest in traumas afflicting previously healthy young men, undermining intrinsic theories of mental illness and arousing psychiatrists' interest in the role of (childhood) traumas in forming the personality. This interest also fit and reinforced the postwar family-centered atmosphere (Grob, 1991).[6]

Bruch's new orientation and change of clientele made her reorient her critique of mainstream American child rearing. This refocus is perhaps best illustrated by the clash between Bruch and the famous anthropologist Margaret Mead over Bruch's child-care manual *Don't Be Afraid of Your Child*, published in 1952. In the book Bruch critiques common pop-psychological advice in which an "unrelieved picture of model parental behavior, a contrived image of artificial perfection and happiness, is held up before parents who try valiantly to reach the ever receding ideal of 'good parenthood,' like dogs racing after a mechanical rabbit" (Bruch, 1952, p. 723).

In a book review, Mead (1954) attacked Bruch for imposing the German ideal of "natural" child rearing on American mothers, who were adopting more liberal ideas to train their children (p. 427). Bruch was infuriated by the review, but the exchange exemplifies how she had begun to take a critical view of mainstream American ways. This critical view was common to many exiled European intellectuals, particularly the Marxists of the Frankfurt school. The echoes of the Frankfurt school in Bruch's work were no mere coincidence either: one of the school's early thinkers, Erich Fromm, was the ex-husband and collaborator of Bruch's analyst, Frieda Fromm-Reichmann.

As in her studies of immigrant children, Bruch turned her attention to parenting when assessing the troubles of her obese and anorexic middle-class patients, except that the set-up and historical situation this time was different.[7] Although anorexia had been "discovered" in the nineteenth century (see Brumberg, 1988), it was a relatively rare and undefined disorder after the war. Some early doctors thought the refusal to eat was a manifestation of female capriciousness. Others understood anorexia to have endocrinological roots, and the early psychoanalysts interpreted it in terms of fear and fantasy of oral impregnation. Bruch discarded the impregnation theory as "mere analogy" (Bruch, 1961a).

The theory of eating disorders that Bruch formulated in the fifties borrowed Erich Fromm's (1941/1965) idea that egotism had its roots in lack of self-love. Fromm argued that this modern lack of trust in oneself resulted from people's freedom from tradition and their enslavement by capitalism, which pitted people against one another in fear of losing their positions. This insecurity that underpinned modern freedom made people both egotistic and pliable at the same time; they were trying to please everyone in order to get recognition and attention. Thus, according to Fromm, capitalism created individuals who were self-centered but lacked self-trust, which manifested itself in increasing social conformism and authoritarianism at the social level (pp. 134–139). Frieda Fromm-Reichmann (1940) modified Fromm's theory and interpreted the person's lack of self-love as resulting from a domineering mother who has made the child doubt him- or herself. Bruch (1961) adapted Fromm-Reichmann's version of the theory and argued that eating disorders had their origin in early feeding experiences.[8] She argued that if the mother responds inappropriately to the child's hunger the child becomes incapable of recognizing her true nutritional needs:

> When a mother learns to offer food in response to signals indicating nutritional needs, the infant will develop the engram of "hunger" as a sensation distinct from other tensions or needs. However, if the mother's reaction is continuously inappropriate, be it neglectful, oversolicitous, inhibiting, or indiscriminately permissive, the outcome for the child will be perplexing confusion in his biological clues and later in his perceptions and conceptualizations. (Bruch, 1961, pp. 470–471)

Bruch concluded that the disturbed feeding patterns set the stage for one's overall inability to recognize one's true needs and to act autonomously. Disturbed eating also becomes a way of coping with the overall psychological problem, and the obese person keeps overstuffing him- or herself to fulfill his or her never appropriately met needs, whereas the anorexic refuses the imposed food as a final but abortive attempt to assert his or her independence (Bruch, 1973).

On one level, just as Bruch shifted the focus from the immigrant children's harsh living conditions to their mothers' attitudes, she reduced Fromm's critique of the psychological repercussions of the exploitative and competitive contemporary society to troubled mother-child interaction. In her therapeutic practice as well as in her writing, this meant dwelling intensively on the patient's interaction with the mother and to a lesser extent on the interaction with other family members.

However, Fromm's original political agenda was not wholly lost in Bruch's work. The middle-class family and its central character, the mother, were a politically loaded subject in the Cold War period. On one hand, the newly affluent ranch-house-and-refrigerator family with its homemaker mother was used as proof of the superiority of the American system of morals, politics, and economics. On the other hand, the suburban home became a source of cultural agony. Amidst early TV dramas that embraced family values such as *Father Knows Best* there were movies that depicted the middle-class home as a loveless place reigned over by passive-aggressive mothers devouring their children, such as the James Dean films. The suburbs, with their box houses penetrated by mass products and culture, were feared to breed a dangerous social conformism, a fascism or communism of sorts (e.g., Skolnick, 1991, pp. 49–74; Susman, 1989). Thus, Bruch's critique of overpowering and frustrated mothers running like mechanical rabbits after the latest child-rearing fad is similar to general contemporary critiques of the suburban household as "a broken home, consisting of a father who appears as an overnight guest, a put-upon housewife with too much to do, and children necessarily brought up in a kind of communism" (Donaldson, 1969, p. 119).

Just like Bruch's portrait of the fat immigrant children a couple of decades earlier, her depiction of the anorexic family reflects central political anxieties of the historical moment. During the post-Depression era the locus of social critique was the newly arrived Eastern European immigrant family that was not able to overcome its traditions and poverty. During the Cold War, the source of anxiety became the expanding, white middle-class, feminized suburbia, which was antithetical both to Bruch's German old bourgeoisie intellectualism and to the rugged individualism held in high esteem in her new home country. Both the theory of obesity and the theory of anorexia presented by Bruch share an anxiety over cultural traits that are perceived to go against the grain of freedom and democracy, even if the content and context of those principles in the two cases is somewhat different.

### On Dependence, Abundance, and Femininity

Bruch developed her theory of the anorexic as a too good middle-class girl in the late fifties and sixties, encapsulating it in her landmark book titled *Eating Disorders* (Bruch, 1973) and in the later best-selling general audience book *The Golden Cage* (Bruch, 1978). In these books she paints a portrait of the anorexic as a too docile girl from an affluent family with a domineering and domesticated mother. In this portrait the girl ends up being too vulnerable to parental expectations of immaculate behavior and performance, and peer pressure and media messages that demand the young woman to be thin and popular. This portrait, which has enthralled the personal and popular imagination on anorexia, resonated with many social, political, and intellectual agendas in postwar America.

Bruch's description of the anorexic as a woman characterized by "cleanliness, no rough play or destructive behavior and no disobedience or talking back," who constantly worries about "not being good enough, not living up to 'expectations' (Bruch, 1978, p. 43), resembles the many scholarly and popular discussions in the fifties about the deterioration of the American character and the rise of authoritarian (Adorno et al., 1950; Fromm, 1941/1965) or "other-directed" (Riesman, 1950/1976) personality. Bruch explicitly links unhealthy behavior with contemporary American culture. This is exemplified in her account of her response to a reporter who asked, "What accounts for the widespread neurosis amongst our children?"

> My spontaneous answer was brief: "The pursuit of happiness and the compulsion to be popular." The interviewer was amazed, even shocked. I was myself surprised but find this brief, pragmatic statement expresses my feeling on the matter even though it needs elaboration. Actually, it is not the *pursuit of happiness* that makes for discontent and neurosis but the way this concept has been transformed into a *demand for happiness*, and the shame of having it known that one is not happy. The compulsive need for popularity is, of course, an expression of the inner uncertainty, that one knows about one's adequacy only by finding acclaim from others. (Bruch, 1961a, p. 224, emphasis in the original)

This argument is nearly identical with Riesman's thesis (which Bruch cites) that Americans had become "other-directed." Riesman held that the new American personality created people who found their direction through their contemporaries, in contrast with the older American personality for which the source of direction was inner (Riesman, 1976, p. 21). Riesman's book evokes a nostalgia for the old American self-reliant personality, a nostalgia that is exemplified by his examples of typical inner-directed characters: "the banker, the tradesman, and the small entrepreneur" (p. 20), mythologized as the bulwark of American liberal democracy and entrepreneurism. Thus, the goody-goody anorexic, in trying to please everyone, becomes not only a symptom of failed infant feeding but represents the fall of traditional American individualism and articulates the Cold War fear of fascism and communism, which pervaded the political spectrum from the right to the left.

Echoing contemporary social critics, Bruch related the anorexic's inadequate personality to the slackening or pathologizing effects of unprecedented postwar affluence and mass culture. Like Riesman, who associated other-directedness with greater wealth and the service and consumer economy, Bruch (1978) linked her patients' illness to their parents' wealth. She depicted the anorexic as feeling trapped in "a golden cage" amongst all the "privileges and benefits" and "luxuries" her parents offered her (pp. 23–24). Furthermore, the anorexic's presumed vulnerability to peer pressure and the "fashion of slimness" "drummed" by the mass media (p. viii) fitted the postwar preoccupation with the possibly dangerous effects of mass media and products, instigated by war propaganda and the spread of mass products to American homes. Thus, the anorexic—presumably fallen ill because of the excess of things and images—became a symbol of popular and academic anxiety with the postwar consumer or mass culture often associated with femininity and its presumed propensity to be seduced or engulfed by objects and irrational desires (e.g., Blackman & Walkerdine, 2000; Bray, 1996; Felski, 1995; Huyssen, 1986; Probyn, 1987).

Overall, Bruch's theories on the relationship between anorexia, which affected predominantly young women, and gender contain a number of contradictions. On one hand, Bruch embraces quite conventional notions of gender. This is evident in, for example, her disapproving comments on her patients' "tomboyish" behavior or "lesbian fantasies" in her notebooks. The same conventional notions of gender are repeated in her published comments about the fat immigrant children's fathers, who could not provide "firm masculine guidance" (Bruch & Touraine, 1940, pp. 167, 176) and her criticisms of the anorexics' mothers, who "while subservient to their husbands in many details," did not "truly respect them" (Bruch, 1973, p. 82).

Yet what has earned Bruch's theory its credentials as (liberal) feminism is her consistent critique of female dependency and domesticity. Bruch argued that the problem with the anorexics' mothers, "women of superior intelligence and education," was that they had given up promising careers or other ambitions in favor of family and children. This only left them unsatisfied. Neurotically focused on their children, they were trying to inculcate them—and especially the anorexic daughters—to live up to their own frustrated dreams (Bruch, 1978, pp. 28–31; Bruch, 1952, p. 155). The anorexic herself "dreaded" the mother's confined life. Yet, trained to be dependent and obedient, she also feared the new demand to "become a woman of achievement in her own right."[9] Thus, Bruch's theory, and many later feminist appropriations of it, renders the anorexic a critical symbol of the tragic threshold, felt with particular acuteness in the sixties, between being pushed back to traditional dependent and docile femininity and being pulled forward toward an independent strong individuality for which women were not necessarily ready.

Bruch's attack on female docility and dependence also articulated a set of broader, contradictory social and political agendas just coming to fruition in postwar America. The theory of anorexia was linked to the fear of social conformism, which leftist intellectuals like the scholars of the Frankfurt school associated with a new type of complacent and conservative middle-class lifestyle. Social conformism was seen to manifest itself in intolerance and hostility toward social critique and reform. However, the fear of conformity was also associated with anti-Communist paranoia and a mixed position looking back to early American culture for its entrepreneurial spirit. During and after the war this agonizing about mass culture mobilized a small army of mainstream social scientists who investigated media effects, public opinion formation, group processes, peer pressure, and the infamous suburbs, all in the name of advancing democracy. Yet as Rose (1996) notes, the subsequent polling industry and social psychological experimentation that were set up to enhance individual freedom and democracy served to perpetuate a normative modern self associated with the social values of postwar America, with all its contradictions.

In Bruch's theory these norms gather around a set of binaries, such as autonomous/dependent, modern/traditional, frugality/luxury, and mind/matter. These dichotomies reflect the division between qualities considered feminine (dependent, pliable, indulgent/consuming, material), and masculine (autonomous, strong, austere/self-controlled, mindful), and they valorize the latter. This normative self is defined in juxtaposition to personal qualities deemed too feminine, particularly the penchant to be too open to or engulfed by other people, (consumer) objects, and ideologies. What

Bruch then seems to suggest is that women overcome their gender in order to attain the normative, rugged, individualist modern self. But Bruch's theories not only suggested a normative psyche but also articulated a strong vision of a normative good society. This good society is decidedly modern in that it has left behind outmoded non-egalitarian ways of thinking, such as traditionalism, and ways of organizing life, such as domesticated femininity. This society would, in principle, allow each individual to live up to his or her full potential, granted that they have the mental strength, independence of mind, and entrepreneurship to make it happen. This description of a good society does not sound very far from the ideal society propagated by contemporary neoliberal governments, where anorexia—an obsession with embodied and intellectual achievement—is endemic.

## *The Spiral of Normativity*

Reading Bruch's work against contemporary discussions on eating disorders, one notices that her original theoretical formulations are still alive, although some of the theories she worked to refute have resurfaced in new disguises and contexts. An association between race and fatness nowadays is evoked to explain why African Americans are fatter than whites. This may be used to raise awareness of the higher risk of cardiovascular disease and diabetes among minorities or to praise the black culture's acceptance or admiration of bigger bodies. Still, theories tracing fatness to race, social class, and lifestyle usually mix into social-hygienic and often derogatory "evidence" of the slackness of the culture of certain groups—not unlike Bruch's comments on immigrant mothers in the thirties. With the completion of the Human Genome Project, interest in the inheritability of obesity has increased again recently, and media these days frequently feature stories on how the "gene for obesity" has been discovered. There is a lively debate on this new "geneticization" of obesity, and it has been suggested it leads to individualization of a social problem (Petersen & Bunton, 2002). Yet, it has also been observed that the genetic theory of obesity currently coexists with a widespread understanding that contemporary society and its lifestyle are at the root of an "obesity epidemic" (Chang & Christakis, 2002). The contemporary public health agenda that both looks for obesity genes and advocates lifestyle change examplifies how models of explanation and intervention that have previously been considered antithetical to each other, such as genetic and behavioral explanations, can come together and produce new hybrid policy agendas.

The psychological theory of obesity, which Bruch advocated early on, continues to be a prominent way through which we make sense of fatness.

The picture of the miserable fat person, gulping down ice cream, candy, and delivery pizzas to assuage his or her personal crises, is present even in productions such as *The Nutty Professor, The Vicar of Dibley* or *Bridget Jones Diaries*, which, in a sense, advocate size acceptance. Eating too much has become an official psychiatric disorder, as binge-eating disorder has been formally included in the latest version of the *Diagnostic and Statistical Manual* (APA, 2004). Bruch pictured the anorexic as a young woman who, made overly docile and dependent by the suffocating family environment, becomes easy prey for the contemporary culture's peer pressure and media imagery. This picture of the anorexic "goody girl" is present almost everywhere eating disorders are dealt with, and has informed media depictions of anorexia ever since the death of the soft-rock singer Karen Carpenter, as will be discussed in chapter 4. It informs Sunday night TV movies such as *For the Love of Nancy* and *Dying to Be Perfect*, and underground films such as *Superstar: The Karen Carpenter Story*, as well as talk shows, psychiatric journals, textbooks, treatment regimes, and feminist research on the condition (e.g., Orbach, 1986).

However, as discussed in the introduction, other feminist works have criticized the idea that the anorexic lacks autonomy. It has been noted that thinness in our culture connotes willpower and independence and that the anorexic may be starving to underline her emancipation and strength (Bordo, 1993). Defining the anorexic as lacking independence may fuel the anorexic's starving, which often is already informed by a desire to attain a free and strong mind, associated with a fit and strong body (Gremillion, 1992, p. 62; Gremillion, 2003; McNeill, 1993). Against the background of my research on Bruch, the self-perpetuating nature of the diagnostic notion of anorexia makes perfect sense. If theories of obesity define fat people as lacking in terms of normative strong and independent individuality, it is logical that anorexics, who starve to ward off negative characteristics associated with fatness, pursue the same strength and independence. It is ironic and tragic that when diagnosed with anorexia, these women are defined as lacking in terms of the very same qualities they were trying to achieve in the first place.

With this irony and tragedy in mind, I have in this chapter aimed to destabilize the normative notions of self and society embedded in Bruch's classical diagnostic discourse on anorexia by demonstrating its dependency on the social structures and issues of a particular moment in time. This does not mean that I would like to denounce Bruch's theories. Rather I have explored their internal contradictions, which emerge from contradictory social developments in the tumultuous post-Depression and postwar years in America. The portraits that Bruch painted of the obese and anorexic delineate what she deemed "pathological" in child rearing, consumption, and self-decoration, and they propagated a certain "modern" lifestyle, personality, and society, independent of mothers, "backward" customs, ephemeral popular ideologies, and the middle-class habit of keeping up with Joneses. Bruch's theories criticized a series of social phenomena that can be considered problematic, such as child beating or the rigid postwar middle-class conservatism and its ideal subordinated femininity. However, her work also rejected behaviors and phenomena considered too foreign or too feminine, and embraced a certain bold individualism, in line with postwar American social values. This line of thinking defines as pathological other modes of being, such as being in relation to, for instance, traditions, customs, (extended) family, or collectives. By saying this, I do not mean to advocate relationality as opposed to autonomy (Gilligan, 1982), which would simply revert Bruch's dichotomy, embracing the negated norm. Rather, I want to draw attention to how modes of being, such as relationality, adherence to tradition and kin, and collectivism, which Bruch deems psychologically and socially dangerous, are usually associated with women, lower socioeconomic classes, new immigrants, and non-Western ethnic groups. The promise of freedom has certainly helped to emancipate some of these disenfranchised groups; yet, it remains blind to the virtues of other modes of being and is also oblivious of the fact that achieving free self-determination is structurally difficult, and in many cases impossible, for social groups that are not bestowed with the privileges of white, wealthy, Western men.

The contradictory social agendas underpinning Bruch's work and the mainstream psychiatric definitions of eating disorders are echoed in the contradictions that characterize the internal universe of women, including myself, diagnosed with anorexia nervosa, as was discussed in the previous chapter and as will be discussed again in chapter 4. Therefore, analyzing the contradictory historical and social underpinnings of discourses on eating disorders helps to make sense of how anorexic women often feel both empowered and shamed by their diagnosis. A historical analysis of Bruch's theories also helps to make sense of the social and political origins of eating disorders. Bruch's descriptions of the lives of fat immigrant children and the lives of her starving anorexic clients illuminate how the changing ways in which we experience ourselves as fat or thin are related to transformations in immigration policy, public health policy, international and military developments, and changes in class and family structures. While this chapter has focused on critically analyzing discourses that define obesity and anorexia, it highlights that if we are to change the ways in which we think and act in relation to our bodies and selves, it is not enough to change how these discourses define eating disorders. We must also address the complex social structures that shape these meanings.

# 4

# *From Autonomy to Flexibility*
## News Discourses on Karen Carpenter and Princess Diana

In chapter 3 I examined the historical, social context that gave rise to the most prevalent understanding of the anorexic as the neurotically perfectionist goody girl. In this chapter I move on to investigate popular representations of eating disorders by analyzing the news coverage of the two most famous women with eating disorders: Karen Carpenter and Princess Diana. As will become evident, there are continuities between the news coverage of the two celebrities and Hilde Bruch's theory, but the discussion will also show that notions of eating disorders do not stay stable but change.

There is an established communications literature on media and eating disorders, which focuses on the gendered politics embedded in the ubiquitous representations of thin female bodies in the media and how this harms audiences, particularly young women (see Wykes & Gunter, 2005). Yet no one has analyzed the gendered politics embedded in representations of eating-disordered bodies and selves (but see Way, 1995). In this chapter I contend that the news stories on Karen Carpenter's anorexia and

---

This chapter was first published as "Rereading Media and Eating Disorders: Karen Carpenter, Princess Diana, and The Healthy Female Self," in *Critical Studies in Media Communication*, Volume 23, Issue 2, 2006, and is reproduced here by kind permission of the National Communication Association, Washington, D.C.

Princess Diana's bulimia promote historically specific normative notions of a healthy female self that are nearly identical to those normative discourses on the ideal female body that fuel anorexia and bulimia.

The news media both eulogized and deplored Karen Carpenter, who died of complications of anorexia in 1983, as an icon of the 1970s sweet, romantic, and feminine soft rock. She was celebrated as a female star and artist with a deep and sophisticated voice, but was also pathologized as an infantile woman with a regressive nonautonomous personality and associated with the reactionary "family values" politics of the Nixon and Reagan era. News coverage of Princess Diana was also double-edged. On one hand, Diana was represented as a classical hysteric slashing herself with penknives and throwing herself down the stairs. On the other hand, she was framed as bursting with positive personal and political female qualities, such as caring and fluidity. Without Princess Diana, those qualities were seen as kept under control under the oppressive, stiff-lipped conservative reign of Margaret Thatcher and the archaic masculinity of the royal beef-eating, fox-hunting, and philandering Prince Charles.

Representations of Carpenter and Princess Diana constructed notions of disordered and nondisordered ways of being a woman. These notions changed over time and were associated with specific historical, social, and political agendas. The story about Carpenter's lack of autonomy framed her as falling victim to the suburban culture and the conservative American family values of the 1970s, values that her soft-rock music embodied. This depiction of anorexia was also very close to the psychiatric theories on anorexia that Hilde Bruch formulated. The coverage of Princess Diana, in contrast, brought into relief the historical contingency of popular definitions of eating disorders. The media representations of Lady Diana Spencer did not straightforwardly reinforce the old, masculine, autonomous self but idealized her feminine fluidity, adaptability, and openness to the world, echoing the values of postindustrial, New Labour Great Britain (see Blackman, 1999; Walkerdine, 1999).

The media coverage of the two celebrities draws attention to, first, the fact that popular discourses on thinness and popular discourses on eating disorders are very similar, fomenting women's anxieties about not being strong and independent enough or not being adaptable and caring enough. Second, the politically invested news stories on Carpenter and Princess Diana underline the influence of broad social structures and agendas—rather than just media enthusiasm with thinness—on popular discourses and attendant behavioral norms on how women should relate to their selves, their bodies, and the world.

## Media and Eating Disorders

To contextualize my analysis of the news coverage of Carpenter and Princess Diana I will review the main contours of communications research on media and eating disorders. Most of this research focuses on media images of thinness and the effects of these images on audiences. For example, classical works in this area have ascertained that Miss America contestants and *Playboy* centerfolds have become slimmer since 1950 (Garner, Garfinkel, Schwartz, & Thompson, 1980; Wiseman, Gray, Mosiman, & Ahrens, 1990). Many studies have tested the hypothesis that such images of thin female bodies have deleterious effects on audiences, particularly adolescent women (e.g. Botta, 1999; Myers and Riocca, 1992, for an overview see Wykes & Gunter, 2005).

In focusing on the correlation between seeing images of bodies of different sizes and self-perception, media scholars have paid scant attention to the contextual factors within which images of thinness become meaningful and acquire their effects. A more contextual approach is offered by feminists. The central argument made by Chernin (1981), Orbach (1986), Bordo (1993), and Malson (1998) is that women's pursuit of slenderness and the images fueling this pursuit articulate a contradictory desire to be both ultrafeminine and masculine. Bordo (1993) argues that depictions of thinness often have an emancipatory flair. Advertisements featuring slender women in business suits or engaged in fitness activities articulate a sense of strength and willpower. They give a new spin to the old associations between femininity and flesh or the body, promising women that they can transcend their feminine bodies, reproduction, and objecthood and attain a mastery of mind over body, a presumably masculine trait. However, Bordo argues that notions of thinness also play into and out of ancient fears of female largeness, hunger, and desire. Thus, being thin or small not only articulates willpower but also diminishes the person, making her less intrusive and less invasive, which conforms to the ideal understated femininity.

Bordo's analysis captures the ambiguities embedded in the ideal thin body between being an active subject and a passive object, masculine and feminine, strong and frail. These ambiguities account for the seductive power of the images and also bear witness to the structural contradictions that shape women's aspirations. However, her work also encapsulates the main dilemma in inquiries into media and eating disorders: In exposing the politics of thinness Bordo yearns for a space beyond the cunning media depictions of slenderness, strength, and suppleness. To illustrate this utopian space Bordo reads Babe—the pig in the children's movie—as an allegory for a transformative self-styling (Bordo, 1997, pp. 62–65). In becoming a sheepdog, Babe adopts a gentle style of herding sheep, which Bordo interprets as a strategy mindful of both difference (between pigs and dogs) and inequality (between pigs, dogs, and sheep). Bordo's rather sweet allegory challenges the contemporary liberalist "you can do it" mentality. This mentality is echoed in media depictions of women engaged in fitness and business activities, which invite women to conform to stale cultural dominants (wear pinstripes, work hard, and be slim) while masquerading as rebellion. Still, her story also reinforces the Cartesian distinction between interior authenticity (being true to pig-style in sheep herding or, perhaps, being true to a feminine, fat, disabled, or black body) and exterior inauthenticity (emulating sheepdogs or body ideals determined by mainstream culture) (see Colebrook and Bray, 1998). In so doing Bordo consolidates the social logic that condemns a bad or disingenuous body or self and endorses a true body or self—a logic that which not only informs studies on the effects of images of thinness but also the starving of anorexics themselves.

Presenting a dichotomy in terms of authentic as opposed to inauthentic generates blind spots in research on eating disorders. The framing of anorexic women as simply sick or under false consciousness contributes to the sense these women have that nobody understands them (Rich, 2006). The sentiment of not being understood also informs the so-called pro-ana Web sites, where anorexic women defend their right to starve as a "lifestyle choice" and display "thinspirational" pictures of their starved bodies. A moral panic has defined these Web sites as sinister and disgusting, and a series of censuring acts, such as their banishment from Yahoo, has forced the sites underground. Closer inspection of these Web sites and communities has revealed that the participants hold an ambivalent attitude towards eating disorders, viewing it as both damaging behavior and a condition to be maintained. Participants in the pro-ana communities also reject definitions of themselves as sick or as mainly starving because of images of models; they define starving in more ambivalent and aspirational terms and view it as a response to deep-seated or serious life disturbances (Fox, Ward, & O'Rourke, 2005; also Mulveen & Hepworth, 2006). Pollack (2003) has also called for a more complex analysis of pro-ana sites and has commented that they should not be denounced as dangerous, but that they should not be romanticized as resistance either. I agree with Pollack. Pro-ana Web sites attack patronizing medical and feminist notions of anorexics as victims of sickness or patriarchy while, at the same time, the Web sites use voluntarist language about starving as a choice, which airbrushes away the structures of inequality that account for why women express their troubles through their bodies.

Popular and scholarly debates over female beauty practices (e.g., the debate between Davis, 1995, and Bordo, 1993, 1997) and eating disorders tend to stall on the question of whether this or that practice articulates *either* freedom *or* oppression ("freedom from dieting" or "freedom to starve"). This tug of war has resulted in an impasse where a *both/and* stance, which would acknowledge how some discourses simultaneously empower and disempower, is impossible. This becomes particularly clear in discussions on pro-ana Web sites, in which ambiguities are seldomly acknowledged. The stalemate results from a simplistic way of conceptualizing the relationship between the self/body and the society and the way in which discourses mediate this relationship.

Some feminist poststructuralists have noted that while biomedical discourse locates the problem of anorexia in individual women's psyche, feminist critiques often locate it in external discourses, which are understood to inscribe their messages onto the women's body/self (Lester, 1997). Feminist criticisms of beauty ideals may underscore that there is no "outside" to historical discourses (Bordo, 1997, p. 189). Yet they leave the interior/exterior relation unformulated, producing an unstated yearning for shaking off the false consciousness perpetuated by oppressive discourses and for being truer to an authentic way of being—as articulated by the metaphor of the piglet being true to her pigletness.

To get over this impasse, scholars (Bray, 1996; Colebrook and Bray, 1998; Eckermann, 1997; Lester, 1997; also Gremillion 2003, from a narrative therapy perspective) have suggested reconceptualizing anorexia using poststructuralist insights from Foucault and Deleuze. Deleuze has reformulated the interior/exterior problematic haunting conceptualizations of subjectivity by suggesting that the self is formed through "folding in" outside discourses (Deleuze, 1988; for a feminist rendition see Probyn, 1993). This focus on the interface between the interior and exterior avoids locating agency within the subject and subjugation outside of the subject, drawing attention to how the self is thoroughly formed by social discourses. This formation is not passive but is an active process whereby the subject incorporates (or folds in) discourses into itself. Foucault's aim was to conceptualize a practice that enhances awareness of the discourses that constitute our selves and facilitates a more active self-construction (Foucault, 1984a, p. 50). This liberatory thread in Foucault and Deleuze is not, however, predicated on a notion of freedom from discourses; as Foucault states, "these practices are not something the individual invents by himself," rather they are "patterns that he finds in his culture, his society and his social group" (Foucault, 1988, p. 11). Critical self-construction thereby refers to an active and alert engagement with social discourses, wherein one weighs their possibilities and pushes their limits rather than reaches beyond them.

Relinquishing the distinction between harmful exterior social discourses and interior authenticity paves a way for a continuing critical engagement with all discourses that invite us to certain subject positions. In research on media and eating disorders, it suggests a critical investigation not only of discourses that propagate thinness (supposed seedbeds of harmful inauthenticity) but also of discourses that explain and lament the prevalence of eating disorders (often presumed to be on the side of more authentic ways of being a woman). An indication that media discourses on eating disorders are presumed to be emancipatory, or at least unproblematic enough not to warrant further inquiry, is that no one has analyzed them (but see Way, 1995). I will begin to shed light on this blind spot in communications literature by analyzing the news coverage of the anorexia and bulimia of the mega-celebrities Karen Carpenter and Princess Diana.

## *Two Female Icons*

Initially my project of examining contemporary representations of eating disorders involved collecting newspaper and magazine articles, films, tapes of television programs, and popular books on anorexia and bulimia. It soon became clear that there was too much material for any in-depth analysis. A mapping exercise helped me to identify celebrities as an important conduit through which stories on eating disorders were conveyed, because they often offer points of emotional identification. For example, after the death of Princess Diana many women grieved her because they perceived her as "ordinary" or "like me" (Blackman, 1999).

Karen Carpenter and Princess Diana are also worth studying because of the attention they brought to eating disorders. Carpenter's death in 1983 noted the first time that anorexia made it to the public consciousness in a major way. Similarly, Princess Diana's revelations about bulimia in the 1990s publicized that condition. I also chose to examine the coverage of Carpenter and Princess Diana because they express different historical time periods, and refer to different social, political, national, and therapeutic agendas. Karen Carpenter's career in the 1970s and her death from complications of anorexia coincided with the reigns of Richard Nixon and Ronald Reagan in the United States. Moreover, her innocent, soft pop as well as her personal affinities with the Republican Party—her husband for a brief period, Thomas Burris, was Reagan's financial aide—associated her with their neoconservative "family values" agenda. Lady Diana Spencer's years as a princess and, later, as an outspoken divorcée coincided with

Margaret Thatcher's reign in the United Kingdom and the landslide victory of Tony Blair's New Labour Party in 1997, and Diana is often associated with this epochal shift in British politics.

Karen Carpenter was treated for her eating disorder by the American psychiatrist Steven Levenkron, who had written a popular book on anorexia titled *The Best Little Girl in the World*. Carpenter became interpreted through Levenkron's classic interpretation of anorexia, which is close to Hilde Bruch's theory on the anorexic as an overly obedient goody girl, as discussed in chapter 3. Princess Diana was treated by the famous English feminist therapist Susie Orbach, who has authored several books on eating disorders, including *Fat Is a Feminist Issue* and *Hunger Strike*. Subsequently, the news media often interpreted Diana's bulimia through the lens of feminism. I take note of the differences between representations of anorexia and bulimia (Burns, 2004), but I contend that the different historical and political contexts account for the differences in the coverage of the two celebrities, even if these differences may come into sharper relief because Karen Carpenter was anorexic and Princess Diana was bulimic.

## Methods

To identify key moments in the media coverage of eating disorders and the two celebrities, I used the LexisNexis database to trace fluctuations in their coverage in major U.S. and U.K. newspapers, newswire stories, and news broadcast. Between 1981 (when the database starts) and the end of 2004, there were 549 articles on "Carpenter and anorexia" and 1673 articles on "Princess Diana and bulimia," with Carpenter attracting more coverage in the United States and Princess Diana more coverage in the United Kingdom. The LexisNexis database from the 1980s is more limited than that from the 1990s, so the magnitude of the coverage of the two celebrities cannot be compared. Yet the database can be used to trace peaks in reporting.

Speculations about Karen Carpenter's thinness and health began appearring in the press in 1975, when she collapsed onstage, but the fact that she had anorexia nervosa became widely known only after her death. Thus the coverage of Carpenter and anorexia first peaked when she died in 1983 (42 articles, in comparison with 3 in 1984). The second peak was in 1988–1989 (15 articles in 1988 and 23 in 1989, in comparison with 5 in 1987 and 15 in 1990), when two films on her came out: *The Karen Carpenter Story*, produced by Karen's brother Richard Carpenter, and *Superstar: The Karen Carpenter Story*, directed by Todd Haynes. The third peak in the coverage was in 1996 (80 articles, in comparison with 14 in 1995 and 38 in 1997) when her posthumous solo album titled *Karen Carpenter* was released.

Journalists began speculating about Princess Diana's eating disorder soon after the birth of Prince William in 1982, but the princess's bulimia became widely known through Andrew Morton's sensationalist biography *Diana— Her True Story* published in 1992 (Morton, 1992/2007). The first major peak in the coverage of Princess Diana and bulimia was in 1995, when she gave her famous *Panorama* interview. In the interview she talked about her bulimia and unhappy marriage (270 articles in 1995 in comparison to 82 in 1994 and 103 in 1996). The second peak was in 1997, after her death (together with lover Dodi Al-Fayed) in a car crash in Paris (350 articles in comparison to 137 in 1998). The last peak in news stories on Princess Diana and bulimia occurred in 2004 when tapes she had recorded for Andrew Morton for her biography and for her voice coach were broadcast on the American television channels CBS and NBC (125 in comparison to 41 articles in 2003).

The peaks in the news coverage of Carpenter and Princess Diana illuminate intense moments in the two women's lives that were deemed newsworthy, either because they were sensational or captured the signs of the times or both. Discussing the peaks in the coverage of anorexia and bulimia from 1983 to 2004 as connected to these two women also allows for documenting historical shifts in the narratives on celebrity and eating disorders during the past two decades.

## *A Fresh Sound and a Somber Note*

The obituaries published immediately after Karen Carpenter's death on February 4, 1983, mostly reflected on her career, which was associated with the comeback of a soft, romantic, feminine rock in the 1970s. This was illustrated in the opening paragraph of the Associated Press's newswire copy on the day she died:

> Singer Karen Carpenter, who with her brother Richard helped bring romance back to pop music in the 1970s with mellow songs like "We've Only Just Begun" and "Close to You," died of cardiac arrest Friday at age 32. (Antczak, 1983)

The romantic, mellow, or soft tone of the Carpenters was frequently given a political spin, with references to its antithetical relationship to the sixties' radicalism and its "hard" music, as illustrated by the same AP news report:

> The Carpenters, whose bright smiles and youthful looks personified their fresh sound, recorded back-to-back hits "Close to You" and "We've Only Just Begun" in 1970. These came at a time when

pop music was dominated by anti-war and anti-establishment themes and hard rock sound. (Antczak, 1983)

Thus, from the very start major news outlets' references to "mellow" and "freshness" in relation to Carpenter and anorexia were double-edged. On one hand, the obituaries eulogized the youthful, dreamy, and phenomenally successful style of the Carpenters. On the other hand, these qualities became associated with tragedy and acquired a darker meaning. Being middle-class and being good or perfect, characteristics associated with the Carpenters, were often conflated with the diagnostic criteria of anorexia; clinicians whom reporters contacted to define this "new" condition to their readers often commented on this link:

> [Carpenter] suffered from anorexia nervosa, a disease that typically strikes weight-conscious teenagers and develops into a potentially fatal obsession that starves its victims. . . . Most anorexics are teenage girls from middle- and upper-class backgrounds. "Most of the people who have the condition are perfectionists," [Dr. Marvin] Gillick said. "The girls who have the disorder are frequently energetic—even though their body is wasting away they are bubbling with energy." (Goulding, 1983)

Two threads, which speak to different social discourses or sensibilities, emerged from the early coverage of Carpenter's death. The first thread, drawing its power from traditional ideals of innocent youth with its conservative undertones, paid tribute to Karen Carpenter's achievements as an icon of the 1970s romantic, melodic popular music. She was associated with freshness and youth and stood in opposition to the masculine, rough, hard rock, associated with political protest and the drug culture of the era. The second thread closely followed the psychiatric theory of anorexia and framed Carpenter's death as a tragedy, rather obliquely associating it with her success, attractiveness, middle-class background, and popular music—all characteristics that fit the diagnostic description of the anorexic as the privileged girl who falls victim to familial and media pressures to be good and thin (Bruch, 1978). The nostalgic and tragic threads were already present in the news coverage by major U.S. media following Carpenter's death, although the immediate obituaries were discreet and fairly uniform. The two threads laid the foundation to the both contradictory and coherent axis around which popular discussion on Carpenter and anorexia revolved and which accounted for the discussion's multidimensional appeal.

## Karen Carpenter: Two Stories

Six years after Karen Carpenter's death two films on her life were released. In 1988 an animation directed by Todd Haynes, *Superstar: The Karen Carpenter Story*, began circulating in the United States. Haynes used Barbie dolls as puppets to enact the story. The film was soon withdrawn from the market, as Haynes had used the Carpenters' music without permission, and it became a hard-to-find underground classic. It was passed from hand to hand among film enthusiasts and later was occasionally available on the Internet. On January 1, 1989, *The Karen Carpenter Story*, a made-for-television movie starring Cynthia Gibb and produced by Karen's brother Richard, was aired on CBS.

The Barbie-animation received significantly less attention in mainstream news outlets than the made-for-television movie, but newspaper reviews enthusiastically embraced its radical political message and avantgardist representational techniques. A column in the liberal-leaning *Washington Post* stated:

> Today Karen Carpenter is fashionable again, the subject of a recent tv-biography and a far more fascinating 43-minute docudrama, Superstar . . . Who could imagine feeling empathy for Barbie or finding depth in the Carpenters' "Rainy Days and Mondays"? . . . The coarse grain of the film and the rigidity of the Barbies impugn the popsicle optimism of the Carpenters' soundtrack, just as Karen's anorexia nervosa destroyed her image as the girl in the split-level next door. And beyond all this, Haynes would show us a pop culture of American Clean that cloaked the corruption of the period. As the Barbie Karen coos "We've Only Just Begun," bombs fall on Cambodia on the television news, part of a series of montage interspersed into the doll docudrama. (Kempley, 1989)

The major U.S. news coverage of the TV movie emphasized the "tragic" elements of Karen Carpenter's story, conveyed by human interest interviews with Richard Carpenter and Cynthia Gibb:

> Cynthia Gibb believes she will never be asked to play as eerie a role as she does in "The Karen Carpenter Story." . . . "Richard (Karen's brother) was on the set every day. Sometimes he appeared to feel great and at other times I could see the strain. But I believe the picture is a catharsis for him and Mr. and Mrs. Carpenter." (Scott, 1988)

Some news outlets reviewed the movie in a critical tone, arguing it had sanitized Karen Carpenter's life story. In part, the *New York Times* review read:

> In the early 1970s, the Carpenters—Karen and her older brother, Richard—began moving to the top of the pop-music charts with a series of easy-listening hits. Clean-cut and only in their 20's, they were the Ken and Barbie of pop music. Let Elvis and the Rolling Stones do their shake, rattle and roll. . . . On CBS at 9 o'clock tomorrow night, "The Karen Carpenter Story" is another of those made-for-television movies that use fact but manage to keep more unsettling truths at arm's length. (O'Connor, 1988)

These quotes illustrate that the posthumous media representations of Carpenter were more clearly double-edged than the obituaries. Particularly the mainstream press focused on the personal and familial tragedy of her death, but the reviews of the TV movie directed by Richard Carpenter often criticized it for censoring the dark side of Karen Carpenter's life, which had led to her anorexia. The press also framed the film directed by Richard Carpenter as low culture by emphasizing its nature as a made-for-television movie and contrasting it to the artsy Barbie animation, just as it classified Karen Carpenter's music as superficial with no "depth," as stated in the *Washington Post*. The coverage of the two films also weaved a story about the dysfunctional and overpowering nature of Karen Carpenter's immediate family, particularly her brother Richard. This was in tune with the common explanation of anorexia as having its roots in suffocating family environment.

The liberal press in particular emphasized Todd Haynes's political interpretation of Karen Carpenter's anorexia as symptomatic of the repressive nature of U.S. global dominance, 1970s and 1980s neoconservatism, and submissive, sweet femininity, which all formed part and parcel of the Carpenters' trademark. Yet, this critical agenda was undercut by the sexist framing of Carpenter in terms of infantile and pretentious femininity—constructed through the continual use of gendered denigrating language, such as "popsicle optimism" and "cooing," emphasis on the softness and shallowness of the Carpenters' music and juxtapositions to the "rattle and roll" of real rock's rugged masculinity. Thus Carpenter's death from anorexia was harnessed to reveal the psychologically and politically repressive underside of 1970s political neoconservatism. Yet, this anticonserative agenda ended up affirming the classical associations between femininity and a regressive or immature personality and reactionary politics (see also Bray, 1996; Probyn, 1987).

## Silenced Voice

In 1996 Karen Carpenter's solo album was released. The media reception of *Karen Carpenter* was contradictory. On one hand, the solo album, which had been shelved after being produced in 1979, was framed as Karen's aborted declaration of independence. Many news reports focused on the production of the album, which was shrouded in controversy, by drawing on interviews with Phil Ramone, the producer who helped Karen to go solo, and his wife Karen Ichiuji. An example is this story from the Labour-leaning English broadsheet *Observer/Guardian*:

> There were glam photo sessions for the album cover. Previously Carpenter had been photographed in matching outfits with her brother. When she saw the proofs of one shot, which showed her elegantly coiffed-up, made-up, and wearing an oversize, white sweatshirt, she ran to Ichiuji in a rare outburst of self-worth. "Look at me Itch," she said. "I'm pretty, I'm really pretty." After four or five songs had been completed she flew back to Los Angeles, tape happily in hand. "She was so in awe of Phil and these cool, hip musicians, who were treating her like an equal," [Frenda] Franklin [Karen's friend] says. "She wasn't used to that." (Richard Carpenter told [Karen's biographer Ray] Coleman that he sometimes wouldn't even tell Karen what she was going to sing until she got to the studio.) (Hoerburger, 1996)

In these reports Carpenter's attempt to perform solo and sing more mature or daring songs (three of the songs were disco) symbolized her desire to become an independent person and to break free of her oppressive familial and professional environment, which were hinted to have contributed to her anorexia. This independence was stopped in its tracks by her brother Richard.

On the other hand, the reviews of the album were mixed. Some reviewers complimented the album, which mixed bluesy tunes with disco and pop, for "leaving modern listeners impressed at her musical breadth" (*Baltimore Sun*, October 10, 1996). Many reviews, however, argued the solo album merely continued the soft pop that was the trademark of the Carpenters:

> In an attempt to prove that America's sweetheart was a full-grown woman, many of these songs make references to the wild thing, combining equal parts wide-eyed innocence and unadulterated

smarm. The total effect is like Lip Smackers crossed with musk oil. The recording is not timeless in any sense, but it does work as a strange period piece, representing the worst of an era. Punk never rears its head in this late '70s pop world filled with lite-music. There's lite-funk, lite-folk, lite-pop. Even the disco is of the lite variety. (Dickinson, 1996)

The coverage of the release of Karen Carpenter's solo album followed familiar tracks. She was both eulogized as a famous, talented female artist and deplored as a representative of "smarmy" lite-music, the antithesis of art. Psychologically, Carpenter is represented as a woman controlled by outside forces, such as her brother and her record company, which chose the music she played and the clothes she wore. At this time, thirteen years after her death, it had also become apparently impossible to write about Carpenter without juxtaposing her feminine musical sweetness and lightness against masculine heaviness—as in punk.

Overall, the news coverage of Karen Carpenter and anorexia drew from and reinforced the psychological notion of the anorexic as a woman suffering from an insufficiently autonomous self (Bruch, 1978). Coverage of Carpenter also built on and reinforced a dominant aesthetic distinction between low and high culture, with the former imagined as feminine and defined as more "mass." Furthermore, particularly the liberal media mobilized Carpenter to make a political commentary on the pathological effects of the 1970s and 1980s American neoconservatism. Together the psychological, aesthetic, and political discourses produced a potent critique of the personally, culturally, and politically repressive elements of the Nixon and Reagan era. The three discourses also represented what was pathological in the psyche, culture, and politics as feminine (see Huyssen, 1986, p. 191). Thus the main message around which popular media discourses on Carpenter converged, and which is close to Hilde Bruch's argument (discussed in chapter 3), was that women should surpass their feminine sweetness, lightness, and softness in order to attain hard or rugged masculine individualism. The liberal feminist declaration embedded in this discourse and the progressive political attack against 1970s and 1980s American neoconservatism and neotraditionalism combined with a sexist eulogy to macho bravado produced a hefty discursive cocktail. Such contradictory discourses may on the surface appear emancipatory, but they often underlie women's troubled relationships with their selves and bodies; they account for the combination of ambitious hubris to achieve and a dark drive to self-destruct characteristic of eating disorders.

## *Princess Diana: Sad or Mad?*

If news coverage of Karen Carpenter lamented her feminine submissiveness, the media career of Princess Diana both celebrated and denounced her feminine assertiveness. By 1995 the marriage of the prince and princess of Wales was in shatters; it came to a culmination in the famous *Panorama* interview, in which Diana noted that "there were three of us in the marriage, so it was a bit crowded." Her reference to her husband's lover, Camilla Parker-Bowles, hinted that Charles might not be suitable as a king. The princess's confession of bulimia, however, became one of the key revelations of the interview. Some newspapers, such as the Labour-leaning *Guardian*, interpreted the revelation through the popular discourse of being a "survivor," such as survivor of breast cancer or sexual abuse.

The discourse of being a survivor celebrates a victim's ability to turn her woundedness into personal strength and political mission (King, in press):

> Her description of bulimia as a survival mechanism was arresting. It became her only means of protest—a survival strategy to which the Palace reacted not with care but with contempt. . . . The Establishment saw it as an attack on the Establishment. They were right. To tell your story is the most dangerous thing to do. Modern movements of survivors, from Siberia to Sloane Square, have redeemed their pain from the psychiatric wards, via the fridge and the phone, the samizdat and the secret services, and transformed it into public, political discourse. Her triumph was her testimony: by bearing witness, she broke the vow of silence that is the perpetrator's secret weapon. (Campbell, 1995)

Other newspapers, such as the conservative *Daily Mail*, harnessed the TV appearance and bulimia to support the claim that Princess Diana was a "basket case":

> Sensing there may be a more fundamental psychological difficulty which accounts for her multiplicity of symptoms, it has been suggested that Diana suffers from a syndrome known as Borderline Personality Disorder. . . . The International Classification of Diseases devised by the World Health Organization declares that for someone to have this problem they must demonstrate difficulty getting on with others, impulsive behaviour, and at least two of the following—profound uncertainty of life goals; liability to become involved in intense but unstable relationships, producing

regular emotional crises; excessive efforts to avoid abandonment; recurrent threats or acts of self-harm; and chronic feelings of emptiness. (Persaud, 1995)

Soon after the interview, Princess Diana's reputation as the friend of the sick and the wretched was further consolidated by her night-time visits to a hospital. This was sometimes interpreted as further evidence of her madness or "compulsive helping" "an addiction to helping others in order to feel needed and loved yourself" (Wrottesley, 1995). Other times the reporters gave the visits a positive spin:

> Princess Diana has been secretly slipping out of Kensington Palace to late-night mercy missions to comfort sick and dying hospital patients. . . . "Some will live and some won't," the Princess says. "But they all need to be loved while they are here." (Brown, 1995)

Like Karen Carpenter, Princess Diana was interpreted in the news as a woman marked by an eating disorder and one who struggled to find herself against the backdrop of an overpowering (royal) family, gendered expectations, and sensational fame. However, the way in which the news outlets wove together the tropes on female madness, gender, and politics in relation to the Princess of Wales was decidedly different from that in the popular discourses on Carpenter. Whereas the posthumous coverage of Carpenter rendered her as exemplifying characteristically feminine psychological and social pathologies, gender acquired a more contradictory meaning in the news on Princess Diana. Diana's descriptions of bulimia were used to interpret her as a classical female hysteric, manifesting the symptoms of borderline personality disorder or compulsive helping. Yet she was also described as a Sloane Square survivor (referring to a London square close to fashionable up-market shops), discharging her female bitterness and energy against the establishment (referring both to the royal family and the conservative, male-dominated culture it represented), while caring, in a decidedly feminine way, for vulnerable groups in society.

## *Transformation and Tragedy*

Princess Diana died on August 31, 1997, and the news media was immediately saturated with biographies evaluating and eulogizing her transformation from a "Sloane Ranger" to the "People's Princess," as the newly elected prime minister Tony Blair named her after her death. *Sunday Mail*'s coverage on the morning after Diana's death was typical:

The world had watched her blossom from a demure, shy 19-year-old into an icon to women everywhere. Diana transformed herself into the most modern, popular and dynamic royal ever. She developed fantastic style, and split her time between the young sons she idolized and the charities and humanitarian issues she dedicated her life to. (Drury & Nairn, 1997).

Princess Diana's image as the ideal woman and a source of identification for women was reinforced by the popular reaction to her death: the gates of Kensington Palace were flooded with flowers, particularly from women and ethnic minorities. Her appeal to "ordinary" women and the downtrodden was underlined by the press (Blackman, 1999). The princess's sensitivity to common people and their problems, which her confession of bulimia was seen to underline, was emphasized in a CNN newscast, which also associated Diana with antihierarchy and American suspicion of royals:

Siobhan Darrow, London: Yes, well, she was certainly a controversial figure, very well-loved here, but one of the reasons she was so controversial was she really challenged the royal family. She was very different from the usual royal that you have—the royal family tends to be very aloof. . . . Princess Diana came out in an interview just before the announcement of her divorce and spoke publicly about her feelings, about her attempted suicides, about her bulimia, about her suffering, about everyday problems that people endure. . . . and that is something that really challenged the hierarchy here and challenged the status quo. (Cesno et al., 1997)

The news coverage following Princess Diana's death was nearly unanimously positive—much the same way as the coverage of Carpenter after her death was discreet. Critical comments began to reappear later in the year, casting her alleged feminine qualities of vulnerability, consumerism, and caring in critical or ironic light:

She was to be the saint of bulimia and anorexia, of diet and fitness obsessed with adolescence, of marital breakdown, of publicly confessed private misery, of hearts worn on sleeves, of pop, of fashion, and of high-profile globalized goodness. She was to be the saint of a sub-political democracy of feeling, the saint of all those, who through ignorance, failure or injustice, felt left out. (Appleyard, 1997)

As evidenced by the news coverage and noted by feminist commentators, the popular narratives around Princess Diana focused on her primordially feminine fluidity or volatility, her caring nature, her mixing of personal and political, and her vulnerability or woundedness (Blackman, 1999; Braidotti; 1997; Walkerdine, 1999). Whereas the news coverage of Carpenter idealized an autonomous, stable, independent self, news on Princess Diana glamorized her transformation from a demure princess to a modern woman and her ambiguities, including being a modern princess, a classic beauty, lonely, miserable and bulimic, a doting mother, and a caring patron of worthy charities from land-mine victims to people with HIV. The press' celebration of her feminine openness to the world and her caring and vulnerability towards others contradicted the ideal of autonomous or bounded self, which is usually imagined as masculine.

The idolization as well as loathing of Princess Diana's femininity can be read in two ways. On one hand, the way in which the media lauded her femininity is refreshing after the repetitively dichotomous coverage of Carpenter in opposition to hard-core men. Diana brought "soft" values to the public life, attending to "desires, aspirations and emotions" that exceeded and expanded what is allowed in politics (Braidotti, 1997, p. 4). On the other hand, media's fascination with Diana's femininity was symptomatic of the times. Diana's confessions about her bulimia and marital neglect, as well as her self-transformation, fitted the contemporary zeitgeist of self-improvement, according to which "failure and psychopathology can be overcome and transformed en route to self-development" (Blackman, 1999, p. 114). Walkerdine observed that "at the moment of Diana's self-transformation many women were economically as well as domestically and personally having to remake themselves" (1999, p. 103). While Braidotti viewed Diana as a harbinger of the feminization of politics, Blackman and Walkerdine connected her idolization with the feminization of the economy in terms of the acceptance of flexible and part-time labor and a continuous restructuring of the workforce. Diana's death and femininity appeared either as the dawn of a more female-orientated public life or as consolidating a subtly exploitative economic and social regime that presented itself as woman identified.

## *Hysteric and an Icon*

The press coverage of Princess Diana rose significantly again in 2004, mainly because tapes recorded by the princess for Andrew Morton's book and for her voice coach Peter Settelen were purchased by and aired on American television networks. The audiotapes contained already familiar information about the extramarital affairs of both Charles and Diana and the bulimia and self-mutilation afflicting the princess. The publicity focused on the emotionally intense details described in the tapes that had not been conveyed before. The *Sunday People* reported:

> On the tape Diana dramatically claims Charles failed to take her suicide threats seriously. "He said I was crying wolf. So I picked up a penknife off his dressing table and I scratched myself heavily down my chest and both my thighs and there was a lot of blood." (Rousewell, 2004)

These emotional scenes that had long been recounted in news reports and books about Princess Diana were sometimes interpreted as further proof of her having been a "high-maintenance" wife and a hysteric. Tony Parsons, considered as a men's issues writer, said in the British tabloid the *Mirror*:

> I heard extracts of those tapes droning on about all this tired old stuff and thought, "Oh, put a sock on it, woman. We have heard it all before." Diana whined on from beyond the grave and I felt as Charles must sometimes have felt—as though he was being nagged into the ground by this incredibly high-maintenance woman. (Parsons, 2004)

Other news sources interpreted these same emotional revelations and scenes as further evidence of Diana's ability to translate personal wounds into a political statement. This was illustrated by the opening statement of the NBC report about the tapes she made with her voice coach:

> Ann Curry: . . . She was just 31, and already an icon—glamorous and famous beyond all measure. But in 1992 Princess Diana was desperate to become something more. With her marriage and her self-esteem in shambles, Diana was about to learn she could channel pain and anger into action. She wanted to speak for the millions who had no voice. But first, she had to find her own voice. Which she did, with the help of a man who would change her life. Tonight . . . she talks about a simmering rage from childhood that erupted years later. And you'll see her remarkable transformation from royal figurehead to a woman of power and principle. (Curry & Lauer, 2004)

Seven years after her death, the news coverage of Princess Diana had consolidated into the oppositional interpretations of emotional revelations as either signalling hysteria and being high-maintenance or as a feminist political statement. Both interpretations drew heavily on her confessions of both bulimia and other types of self-harm. The negative take focused on her emotional, embodied, and sexual female excess. The positive take interpreted her intense emotionality as a refreshing female force that exposed the personally and politically damaging nature of British conservatism. Yet, particularly in Britain, the media was also beginning to comment on the repetitive and old nature of the Diana story. Her personal, political, and charitable legacy was waning and the press focused on Prince Charles, William, Harry, and Camilla Parker-Bowles.

## Autonomy and Flexibility

Useful here is Martin's (1994) work on changes in the notions of the body, particularly the immune system, in the twentieth century. Martin discusses how the human immune system has traditionally been perceived as a fortress protecting the body from outside invaders. However, the immune system has recently been reconceptualized as an open system; an open system is more able to interact with and adapt to its environment. Martin argues that the new ideal "flexible" body—an idea that saturates contemporary biomedicine, homeopathy, and management theory—seems new and exciting against the ideas about closed bodily borders. Martin argues the new ideal also harbors a type of social Darwinism. Now bodies must be trained to be flexible, responsive to the shifting challenges posed by the environment lest they wither in the turbulent biological and economic context. The news coverage of Karen Carpenter reaffirms the ideal of individual body/self as a bounded fortress, staying true to itself, rather than being pliable to ephemeral outside ideologies and influences. The news on Princess Diana, however, is different in that it clearly idealizes a flexible, fluid, and adaptable body/self, a self that opens up to the world and transforms in tandem with the opportunities and challenges life presents it.

The news coverage of Carpenter and Princess Diana bears witness to the political shift Martin identifies from the ideal of a masculine, bounded autonomous self to an ideal that values feminine openness and fluidity. This also repeats in the therapeutic realm, where psychoanalytic and family systems approaches are complemented with New Age, self-help, art, and adventure therapies. These therapies usually emphasize openness and fluidity of the self.

The analysis of news discourses about Karen Carpenter and Princess Diana draws attention to how not only media images of thinness but also media representations of eating disorders legitimate the same gendered, historical structural contradictions that interlace women's problematic relationships with their body, self, and achievement. Regardless of its critical accents, the news discourse on Carpenter's anorexia basically invites women to annihilate their feminine self, which is found wanting in personal and political terms. The news discourse closely mimics the idealization of thinness and fitness with its references to masculine mastery and self-determination that inform anorexia in the first place. This discourse is similar to Hilde Bruch's classical psychiatric definition of anorexia as symptomatic of a poorly individuated self, and its re-emergence in news coverage of Carpenter and neoconservatism illustrates how psychiatric theories become popular commonsense and get articulated to different political agendas. The news coverage of Princess Diana's life and bulimia, however, speaks in a different voice, drawing attention to the historical contingency of the ways in which we make sense of abnormal eating habits. The press' enthusiasm with Diana's transformations fit contemporary fascination with changing the body and self. However, the quest to transform their bodies and their selves also leads women to dissatisfaction with their selves and to eating disorders.

The news discourse on Carpenter also attacks the American 1970s and 1980s hegemonic conservative consensus, founded on a heteronormative notion of family values, female domesticity, unquestioned global dominance, and a "don't rock the boat" mentality vilifying the 1960s. Princess Diana's partly unruly femininity is refreshing after all the blaspheming of femininity in the coverage of Karen Carpenter. The popular discourse on Diana implies an element of piglet being true to her pigletness or what Bordo (1997) calls transformative self-styling that brings the suppressed feminine to the public domain (Braidotti, 1997). The contradictions of the discourses on Karen Carpenter and Princess Diana highlight their multidimensionality. A tendency in research on eating disorders to classify discourses as inherently emancipatory or damaging is blind to this multidimensionality. Take for example, the sexism that interlaces the critical politics around Carpenter or the dominant economic ideology that underpins the pro-feminine politics around Princess Diana. Nuanced feminist engagement with the symbolic and political struggles that anorexia and bulimia articulate is necessary; neither autonomy nor flexibility is the solution to eating disorders.

# 5

## *Voices and Discourses*

### Layering Interviews on Eating Disorders

One of the main goals of this book has been to argue against the diagnostic logic that defines anorexic women as "outside of the true" or unreliable witnesses of their own experience. This logic leads to reading the anorexic's, such as Karen Carpenter's, words as symptoms of an underlying psychological or social pathology; as symptoms, they must be deciphered by an expert, such as a psychiatrist or even a feminist cultural critic. However, as I discussed in chapter 1, defining someone as disordered allows any ordinary person, including a friend or an acquaintance, to pass judgment on an anorexic's disordered behavior. Research conducted within the diagnostic approach rarely listens to what women with eating disorders are saying but rather tries to fit their words into a predetermined theory or social commentary.

When I initiated interviews with women who had had anorexia or bulimia, I wanted, in a hermeneutic feminist spirit, to listen carefully and be faithful to their voices. However, I also wanted to be able to critically examine the discourses that have defined eating disorders, which form an integral part of the self-understanding of anorexics and bulimics. Thus, when beginning the interviews, I was faced with a methodological dilemma: How to be true to the voices of the anorexic women and, at the same time, critically assess the discourses that form the very material of which their voices are made?

The methodological approach I chose draws on the hermeneutic impulse of being true to the voices or experiences of the people being studied and the poststructuralist interest in analyzing discourses that shape our voices and experiences. This approach draws on various sources, including Ronai's (1998) "layered" account and Denzin's (2002) notion of "cinematic interview." Attentive to both voices and discourses the methodology informs both the way in which I conducted interviews with the women and the way in which I interpreted the interviews afterwards.

Denzin notes that "the interview, whether conducted by social researchers, mass-media reporters, television journalists, therapists, or counsellors, is now a ubiquitous method of self-construction" (Denzin, 2002, p. 833, also Gubrium & Holstein, 2002). I contend that interview-based research on women with eating disorders has often reproduced familiar cultural and diagnostic tropes about women starving because of beauty ideals and lack of independence. I admit that body ideals and issues of autonomy may in many cases motivate women's starving. However, if one listens with a different ear, there are other stories being told and other voices to be heard about eating disorders. Interviews with anorexic women can affirm the familiar tropes about beauty and autonomy, but also violently criticize notions of anorexics as victims of these ideals.

Using their own weapon, the interview, I will complicate the often rather jaded way in which journalists, counsellors, and even social researchers construct the anorexic self.

## *Voices*

Research that aims to be true to silenced or misunderstood voices has its origins in feminist and postcolonical critiques of scientific interest in the experiences of subjugated groups, such as non-Western people, the working class, or women. The critiques have argued that scholarship that focuses on disenfranchised groups often fails to communicate the voices of the disenfranchised. Instead this scholarship is used to support political projects, ranging from colonialism to Marxism and humanist feminism (see Clifford & Marcus, 1986). When studying women with anorexia and bulimia, taking these critiques seriously is particularly important as the women's words are often dismissed as disordered and interpreted to testify for the ills of a variety of social and political developments, as discussed in the previous chapters.

Contemporary research paradigms have developed modes of inquiry that are more sensitive to the experiences of the disenfranchised. Feminist scholars have used part autobiographical and collage-type strategies to give voice to women's and men's rarely discussed experiences, such as domestic violence (e.g., Jones, 2000). Sociologists studying emotions have developed ways of writing and research that convey the intimate and visceral level of taboo experiences, such as abortion or death (e.g., Ellis & Bochner, 1992, 2000), while anthropologists have written self-reflective accounts on the relationships, shot through with inequality, between themselves and their informants (Behar, 1996; Jackson, 1998). Oftentimes these accounts have provided powerful counternarratives to stale dominant descriptions of the experience in question. For example, Jones's (2000) story about the love and violence between a young couple (Andrea and Andrés) challenges the jagged narrative about "martyrs and monsters" that saturates descriptions of violence in relationships and makes it impossible for women and men to recognize themselves in these stories and to begin to address the complexities of the problem.

However, sometimes the quest to be truer to lived experiences frames these experiences as something "genuine" that reveals itself under close inspection, causing the researcher to become blind to the social nature of experiences and their interpretations. This can be seen in Kiesinger's "From Interview to Story" (1998), an evocative narrative that aims to convey the visceral and emotional reality of the painful and stigmatized life of Abbie, a 450-pound bulimic woman. In an attempt to understand what it "means" and "feels like" to be fat, Kiesinger cues on Abbie's body:

> How will I write about an obese life without having lived one? I look at Abbie intently, focusing on the beads of sweat that form on her forehead. I look at her eyes—tiny blue splashes submerged in folds of skin above her cheeks. I note her ankles and feet, pink and swollen . . . I note her attire—a lilac cotton frock with pink trim around the neckline, soaked with perspiration. (p. 83)

Kiesinger's description of Abbie's body is visceral; she is trying to capture that level of experience. Probyn (2000) has noted that the problem with being politically correct about fatness is that it pushes our revulsion and disgust toward bodies deemed grotesque under a "sanitized veneer of acceptance" (p. 128). The strength of Kiesinger's story is that it brings the powerful disgust associated with fat bodies to the fore, powerfully illustrating the pervasive feeling of "shame" that marks Abbie's life. However, the trouble with Kiesinger's introspective description of the shamefulness and painfulness of Abbie's body is that she holds onto it as "real." She does not question the ubiquitous popular, clinical, dramatic, and comedic discourses on the sweaty, swollen, overbearing, and overflowing nature of fat that ground her story. Eventually, even if Kiesinger tries to identify or empathize with Abbie, she ultimately posits Abbie as inferior to, and different from, her self (It must be horrible to be that fat!). Thus, while this mode of research makes its audience face a "different" embodied experience, it does not shatter the audience's sense of their bodies but rather affirms their normality. In the end, the piece ends up repeating the voyeuristic panning of "freak" bodies and people. This is typical of talk shows, which make their audiences laugh and feel good about themselves and their normality in relation to the abhorrent, abject bodies/selves of others. This similarity between sensationalist popular media and unreflective forms of new ethnography or sociology has been pointed out by many scholars and testifies for the strength of dominant social discourses that seem to find a way of recirculating themselves everywhere (Atkinson & Silverman, 1997; Clough, 1997, 2000; Lowney & Holstein, 2000).

## *Discourses*

The other research paradigm that informs my work, poststructuralism, focuses on social discourses that structure personal experiences. In principle, poststructuralism negates the idea of resuscitating a silenced experience or voice. Instead, we experience ourselves as mentally disordered or even as having a life story according to how we subjectify social, historical, and institutional discourses (e.g., Foucault, 1978; Hacking, 1995; Rose, 1999).

There is an established feminist poststructuralist scholarship on eating disorders that investigates the way in which these conditions are informed by problematic social discourses, such as thin beauty ideals and modernist ideals of self-control. For example, Susan Bordo has used the poststructuralist approach to analyze how anorexia embodies a contradictory quest to suppress the "feminine," using quotes from the clinical interviews performed by Hilde Bruch:

> Hilde Bruch reports that many anorectics talk of having a "ghost" inside them or surrounding them, a "dictator who dominates me," as one woman describes it; "a 'little man' who objects when I eat" is the description by another. The little ghost, the dictator, the "other self" (as he is often described) is always male, reports Bruch. The anorectic's *other* self—the self of uncontrollable appetites, the impurities and taints, the flabby will and tendency to mental torpor—is the body as we have seen. But it is also (and here the anorectic's

associations are surely in the mainstream of Western culture) the *female* self. (Bordo, 1993, p. 155, emphasis in the original)

The insight of Bordo's analysis is that it illuminates certain primordial social dichotomies or discourses that interlace not only experiences of eating disorders but Western thought in general. It casts something like Kiesinger's story on Abbie in an undeniably critical light. Bordo's analysis makes it clear that Kiesinger's revelling on Abbie's swollen body parts, folds of flesh, and clothing stained with perspiration is not any kind of "intrinsic" subjective experience but thoroughly embedded in the ancient Western abhorrence of feminine flesh. This accounts for the methodological strength of Bordo's argument, as it draws attention to how our subjective experiences of ourselves is always guided by social discourses that we are not conscious of, or that operate "behind our backs."

However, Bordo's analysis also has weaknesses. Bordo's most obvious methodological shortcoming is that she cuts and pastes snippets of an anorectic's talk from a psychiatric textbook and makes grand conclusions about it. Bordo's reading of the anorectic's speech flattens it into a one-dimensional prop for her theory, reducing the anorexic into a victim of dualism.

In principle, poststructuralism does not necessarily invite such a one-dimensional interpretation but provides tools for a more perceptive questioning of discourses, including ones that frame women as victims. Using a poststructuralist perspective, Malson (1998), for example, has observed that anorexics are often acutely aware that their starving is defined as a sign of vanity or superficiality, which posits them as falling short of the self-governed, controlled, and "depth" masculinity that they are often trying to attain through anorexic practices in the first place (pp. 157–158). Against this, Bordo's representation of anorexics as victims of dualism perpetuates the problem of always framing women as lacking by framing them as primordially feminine "dupes" (also Davis, 1995).

Eventually, even if Kiesinger (1998) and Bordo (1993) approach eating disorders from different directions, their conclusions are similar in that they both presume an unproblematic access to experience. Kiesinger envisions gaining this access through introspective identification with Abbie, whereas Bordo imagines accessing experience through reading internalized social discourses from the words of the anorexic woman. In their different ways neither of them tackles the slippery nature of experience that is shot through with multiple and multilayered discourses. I seek to be sensitive both to the voices of women who have had eating disorders, and to the discourses that interlace their voices/experiences.

## *Voices/Discourses*

Some recent feminist studies have addressed the ambivalence of experiences of eating disorders. Interviews with anorexic women, as well as analyses of posts on pro-ana Web sites, have revealed that anorexics often experience their condition as simultaneously empowering and damaging. Anorexics have also been found to be highly critical of the disparaging and alienating nature of diagnostic discourses that define them as irrational or vain. Such discourses contribute to their sense of alienation in relation to therapists, relatives, and friends and account for the popularity of pro-ana sites, where women with eating disorders feel understood (Fox, Ward, & O'Rourke, 2005; Malson, 1998; Rich, 2006). These studies are ethnographically or sociologically sensitive, capturing the subtleties of their material rather than imposing a one-dimensional pattern on it about anorexics as victims of dualism. However, these accounts obey traditional social scientific conventions of analysis and writing, according to which a detached researcher makes observations on "patterns" in research subjects' speech, even if these patterns are found to be contradictory.

My aim goes beyond this. I start from the premise that both researchers and the people we study are always only partially aware of the ideals and sensibilities that guide our thoughts and actions. Therefore, our speaking or writing always not only articulates our voices but also the discourses that speak through them (Foucault, 1982; Volosinov, 1973). To do justice to the double-sided nature of experience, which comes into particularly sharp relief when studying eating disorders, necessitates taking it into account in the manner in which we conduct our research as well as in the way in which we interpret and represent it.

To make sense of the voices/discourses that interlace our experience of ourselves and others I use Ronai's (1998) heuristic of a "layered account." Ronai notes that minds or selves "retain all the traces or impressions of what has been 'written' there by society," and end up in permanent "dialectic between the input of writing from the external world and the traces of prior impressions from society" (p. 407). The layered account attempts to capture some of these layers of writing that mediate the way in which we perceive our selves and others through the use of sketches and vignettes that are juxtaposed to each other. The aim of the technique is to unsettle preconceived ways of interpreting people or phenomenon by bringing into relief the multiple layers of meaning that sediment any interpretation. This is illustrated in Ronai's description of Kitty, an erotic dancer:

Kitty is cute and curvy. Sexy. She looks like someone who just wants to play, have fun, and be loved.

Kitty is tall, intimidating, built like a fuckin' Valkyrie warrior maiden, ready to swoop down from Walhalla and kick ass.

Kitty is too fleshy for her frame and height. She teeters the line between voluptuous and vulgar.

Kitty is a blatant victim of false consciousness, buying into her own oppression and objectification by reproducing the very images that oppress her.

Kitty is a hard-core feminist who fully embraces her power as a woman.

She is nothing but a tall, tacky, pathetic whore.

Kitty is a business woman who owns a travelling strip show and strip-o-gram service in a major metropolitan area in the southeast region of the country. (Ronai, 1998, pp. 407–408, shortened)

By juxtaposing the various possible interpretations of Kitty, Ronai demonstrates that they each have a kernel of truth to them while being, at the same time, entirely inadequate and stereotypical descriptions of her. Throughout the article about Kitty Ronai shifts between telling what it is like being a part of a traveling strip troop (listening to voices), and drawing attention to the interpreted and mediated nature of her telling so as not to allow her audience to fall back to rehashing their comforting, customary ideas about strippers (unsettling discourses).

The shifting between telling a story deemed important (voice) in a way that is continuously aware of its represented or enacted nature is also typical of so-called cinematic interview techniques (Denzin, 2002; also Minh-Ha, 1989). Ronai's layered account also resonates with Bakhtin's (1981) notion of dialogic or polyvocal novel, which juxtaposes diverse voices to each other to bring to the surface their different social accents or agendas, as we can see in Ronai's descriptions of Kitty.

To operationalize the layered framework I, first, conducted my interviews with women who had had eating disorders in a way that I hope better captured voices and discourses and the fact that we are always partly, but only partly, aware of the dance between the two. In the interviews I first invited the women to tell me their story of anorexia or bulimia, aiming to elicit their "voice." In the second part of the interview I asked them what they thought about medical and popular discourses on eating disorders, in a sense inviting them to do discourse analysis with me. Through this interview strategy I also wanted to problematize the classical division of labor between the researcher and the researched according to which the researched provide the raw speech, from which the voice or discourse is then interpreted by the researcher. To destabilize these roles I solicited the women to partly do research with me, even if ultimately the overall presentation of their stories is in my handwriting.

While my interpretation and writing up of the research was informed by Ronai's notion and example of layering, my account is layered differently. I sought to both capture and deconstruct the experience of the people I was studying not only by interrogating my own interpretations but also by inviting the women I interviewed to both convey and deconstruct their own experience for or with me. Thus, I sought to unsettle preconceptions about anorexics by first juxtaposing the women's accounts of their experiences of eating disorders to one another. This first layer of voices/experiences complicates classical notions of anorexics by exposing not only the similarities between the accounts but also differences between them. Second, I juxtaposed the women's assessments of the ways in which women with eating disorders are represented. The second layer of voices/discourses/interpretations unsettle classical notions of anorexics by showing how they can be experienced as true, as lies, as irrelevant, illuminating, and violently insulting, or all or some of these things at the same time.

The layers of interpretations of experience and interpretations of interpretations complicate customary ways of thinking about what is wrong with women with eating disorder and how they should be treated, both clinically and socially. These multilayered stories relate personal stories and views, but also connect with the preceding chapters of the book as they illuminate the social processes and structures that speak through these accounts. These processes and structures are revealed not to be uniform but many and contradictory.

Despite my emphasis on being sensitive to the multiplicity of voices/discourses, I found that the women's stories shared one important thing in common: The women I interviewed, who had recovered from an eating disorder, had all adopted a self-reflective life philosophy that was ambivalent about all social (media, parental, sports, educational, medical, etc.) discourses that suggested to them who they should be. I contend that this attitude to life and various social invitations to lead one's life in a particular way represented a hard-won truth that these women had discovered after often a long journey through the blind alleys of starving, self-improvement, self-depreciation, and unsuccessful treatments. This ambivalence had often been integral to these women's personal healing. In this chapter, I hope to simulate the women's attentiveness to the many-sided nature of discourses that promise to lead to happiness, excellence, health, and freedom. Too often research on eating disorders ends up an accomplice to the judgmental attitude toward the gendered body/self that informs eating disorders. My aim is to experiment with representing women with eating disorders in a way that goes against this logic.

## *Complicating Eating Disorders*

The following discussion is based on four in-depth interviews with women who each had had an eating disorder. The interviews were conducted in the late 1990s, and at that time the women were between 20 and 35 years of age and were all studying for an undergraduate or postgraduate degree at a university. Three of the women had primarily had anorexia and one of them had had bulimia, and they had each experienced the eating disorder as a teenager or young adult. Two of the women were American and two of them were Finnish. At the time of the interviews the women were no longer acutely starving or bingeing and purging and described themselves as more or less recovered. The women were my friends, acquaintances, or friends' friends. Because they all came from my social circle, they were a lot like me: white, heterosexual, well-educated, and mostly from the middle class.

I purposefully interviewed women who would fit the image of the prototypical woman with an eating disorder in terms of being white, high-achieving, and privileged. I did not interview these women in order to argue that their accounts would be representative of stories of anorexics more generally. Rather, I wanted to interview "prototypical" anorexics in order to ask them what they thought of discourses on prototypical anorexics, which presumably describe them. I also interviewed women in my social circle because it enabled me to get in touch with women outside of a treatment setting. I did not want to interview women in treatment, as I was concerned this would focus the conversation on how to achieve recovery. I also chose to talk to recovered women, thinking they would be in a better position to reflect back on the experience and on the discourses that had influenced them before and after the diagnosis.

I first describe the four women's accounts of having an eating disorder. In the subsequent section I discuss their views on discourses on eating disorders. All the names used are pseudonyms, and some personal details have been changed to protect anonymity.

## Creating a New Self

### Jeanne

When I interviewed Jeanne she was in her early thirties and was working on a PhD in social sciences. Jeanne was American, and she interpreted her undergraduate years, when she was anorexic, as symptomatic of the "Reagan years":

> This was when women were supposed to have it all, be extremely successful in all realms and be extremely thin and good-looking, and I took that to heart in a really dangerous way. So, I found myself more and more obsessed with eating less and less, and I exercised a lot too. I would make myself run and run and run and run, and even though I felt like shit and had no energy, you know, I'd force myself to do this.

Jeanne told that she also worked in popular campus bars, where her body was constantly on public display, and she used the money she made to buy fashionable clothes, such as short tops, to show off her thin body. She was also a good student and, in general, consciously pushed herself in every way she could:

> I would go to the undergraduate student lounge, where people could smoke. And I'd smoke, smoke and smoke and drink diet sodas and just study into the night. It was just this form of personal hell, but I enjoyed knowing I was getting all my homework done and wasn't slacking off.

### Taru

Taru, the second woman interviewed, was in her early twenties and studying social sciences at a Finnish university. She had been anorexic in her teens and associated her starving with having danced ballet competitively. Taru explained that she first began to lose weight to hide a technical flaw:

> I used my muscles in a wrong way, and it was really taxing on my muscles and joints and everything. I knew that already when I was very little, like twelve years old. I thought, these people think I am doing it right, but I knew I wasn't doing it right. . . . When I started to develop a bit, I just felt that I could hide this flaw better if I was lighter. So, it just started from trying to hide the fact that my tech-

nique was not perfect. [Translated from the Finnish language, hereafter TFL]

Being light was of primordial importance in ballet and Taru remembered how she felt superior in relation to the other girls:

> After Christmas we were told to look into the mirror, and the teacher announced that there was only one girl in the class who looked the same as before Christmas. I always knew it was me. . . . Then Laila [the teacher] held a stick up and asked the other girls to jump over it, commenting like: "See, how difficult it is to jump with all that mass." . . . I took this as indirect praise for me; I thought, I do not have to be subjected to something like that because I do not have a problem. [TFL]

Taru recounted how for fifteen years, from the age of 5, she did everything she could to become a professional dancer. She put herself through an excruciating regime of endless exercises, pain, long stays abroad, crossing half of Finland to go to lessons. She used to carry a plastic container with five deciliters of boiled rice and Tabasco sauce. "It was my daily food portion. Every now and then I would dip into the container and take a forkful of rice, it was so hot it felt warm in the stomach," she said.

## *Eleanora*

When I interviewed Eleanora, she was also in her 20s and studying social sciences at a Finnish university. Eleanora had developed anorexia in her teens, and she had also experienced occasional binge eating but not fully blown bulimia. When Eleanora was 6 years old her mother, who had been diagnosed with schizophrenia, committed suicide. This cast a shadow over Eleanora's childhood, and left her feeling alone and abandoned:

> I felt terribly abandoned. And I unconsciously blamed my mother a lot. I felt that she had abandoned me, and my father had abandoned me, and my sister had abandoned me. I felt that nobody was with me. I don't blame them (my family) for anything anymore; they had their own lives to mend. But because I was so little, I missed caring so much. [TFL]

When Eleanora was in her teens, the pain and loneliness broke out in her starving. She decided that she wanted to "improve" herself and become beautiful. "I wanted to be beautiful and thin, so that everyone would love me," she said.

At the time of the interview, Eleanora was in a relationship with a young Finnish man, Jarmo. She told how Jarmo cuddled her and caressed her and told her that he loves her. Eleanora enjoyed this, but it was not wholly unproblematic:

> I absorb [Jarmo's tenderness] like a sponge. But when he went away for a few days, I found myself consoling myself by buying a bag of sweet licorice and eating them all at once. And I felt so disappointed with myself for doing that, disappointed that I have become emotionally dependent on a man and cannot live up to my totally exaggerated ideal of being an independent woman. [TFL]

Eleanora explained she had struggled with a desire to be independent and loved throughout her life. She said that when younger, her fear of being abandoned made her turn difficult whenever she was becoming close to someone, as she felt they would soon leave her. At the time of the interview Eleanora was going through a bad patch with Jarmo, who was not happy about her plans to go traveling without him. "He does not understand how fully independent I am; it would never occur to him to travel alone," she said.

## Crystal

When I interviewed Crystal, an American woman, she was in her early 30s. She had recently completed her doctorate and was moving to another state to take up her first clinical job. She had obtained an undergraduate degree from Yale and then received a master's degree in nutrition. She was the only one of the women discussed in this chapter who was bulimic. Crystal associated her bulimia with having become a vegetarian when very young:

> I guess I always was a weird eater, 'cuz I never liked the taste of meat. So pretty young, like thirteen, I started cooking for myself, because I didn't like meat. And I started going to the health food stores, because I needed to find out how to feed myself without getting weak. When I first started out, I would eat noodles . . . that's all I would eat for weeks, pretty unbalanced. But then I also learnt about economic and political and other good reasons to be vegetarian, so it became a little bit more politicized. But the bottom of it is that I just didn't like meat. So I started eating all kinds

of weird foods, weird for a high-school context. Like eating tofu was pretty weird back then.

Crystal explained that she was in a "fog" about how and exactly when she became bulimic, but her interest in food and bulimic roommates played a role. When asked about the political side of her eating, Crystal became animated and explained that "if you took all the grains that we feed to cows, and fed it to humans, there would be a lot less starvation." "And there are all these issues, like how food is radiated . . . and it becomes an economic argument, but then it's also a health issue," she continued.

Crystal also associated her bulimia with her attempt to numb her feelings, particularly anxiety, which were never dealt with in her family or elsewhere (on the numbing effect of bingeing and purging, see Malson, 1998, p. 168). To illustrate what she meant, Crystal told how when she was an undergraduate at Yale she got writer's block:

> And I just went nuts. I was walking around the campus in circles. And I wound up wandering into my apartment, and my roommate found me and cleverly walked me over to the health services. They plunked me in a bed. And then they just basically took care of me, and I wrote my paper in bed. And I got an A. But then, afterwards, no one dealt with it. They kicked me out, no follow-up, no nothing.

Crystal started recovering from bulimia after attending a self-help group organized by a woman named Lisa, who had herself been bulimic. Lisa was feminist, having been politicized by her bulimia. She was the first one to address Crystal's suppressed anxiety and other emotions. She helped Crystal begin to address the "enormous pressure" she was sensing from Crystal having to do with Crystal's Yale background and applying to medical schools.

## *The Four Women*

Analyzing the accounts of the four women, it seems that they all had initially begun to starve to create a new, better, more successful, flawless, attractive, lovable or altruistic self/body. It has been suggested on theoretical (Bray, 1996; Lester, 1997) and empirical (Malson, 1998) grounds that anorexia should be conceptualized as an attempt to fetch a new self or, to use Foucault's terminology, practice of the self (Foucault, 1985a, 1985b). Conceptualizing anorexia this way acknowledges the strong aspirational component of eating disorders rather than viewing them as mere subjugation.

Jeanne, Taru, Eleanora, and Crystal had all begun starving in order to excel in something—school, dance, looks, or politics. While their quests are not surprising against the literature on eating disorders, their projects, such as being successful in school or sports or becoming a vegetarian to address world hunger, do not simply articulate sexist or reactionary agendas. Each of the women was critically aware of the problematic nature of the social goals that had driven her to starving, and each had concluded that what had seemed like a good idea initially had a problematic underside, even if most of them had reconsidered rather than wholly rejected their original goals.

In addition to the similarities between the stories, there are also differences. Whether it looks like the stories form a clear pattern or form something more like a complex mosaic depends on the angle in which they are viewed. One of the women was driven to starve because of a tragic personal history—a mentally ill mother committing suicide—while others were informed by diverse social agendas, from the individualism of the Reagan years to a political quest to address world hunger and ecology through personal food choices or to conform to the contrived body ideal dictated by classical ballet. Eating disorders may generally highlight the fact that women seem to express various social and personal goals and problems through bodily practices, which may be a useful starting point for making sense of the gendered nature of the condition. However, in light of just these four interviews, we can see how drawing broad generalizations about how women with anorexia or bulimia are driven by beauty ideals or gender identity glosses over many other important issues women relate to their starving. Such glossing contributes to anorexic women's sense of alienation or their sense that nobody understands them or the "real" reasons behind their starving (Malson, 1998, Rich, 2006).

## *Reflecting on the Anorexic Self*

### *Jeanne*

When, in the second part of the interview, I asked Jeanne what she thought of theories of anorexia, she replied that she was "a textbook case." She had been a middle-class, white girl from an affluent community and with well-educated parents. Jeanne continued that she admitted that anorexia can be "serious and life threatening" and that having gone through it, she felt sympathetic towards people who have been "vulnerable to cultural norms as she was." Yet she stated that she still felt uncomfortable about having had it:

> I think that, you know, it's hard not to hierarchize mental problems and psychological difficulties. But now it seems to me to be just so self-indulging, it's like such a, I don't know, I still wrestle with that. I mean, in a lot of ways I don't like the fact that I had it. I would feel like it was better if I would have had something that I couldn't control at all like schizophrenia.... It just seems so like something that I did to myself and stupidly made it worse and worse and worse.

Jeanne was a feminist and also active in other progressive political projects. She felt that she had been "stupid" for having been fooled into starving and self-centered individualism, but she also acknowledged the experience had consolidated her feminist consciousness and made her more understanding of people vulnerable to outside influences. Jeanne's interpretation of anorexia as self-indulgent was not only her own conclusion but was shared by several important people around her. Her second therapist had been very "cold" or "nonplussed" in her dealings with her. Jeanne said she could understand her, because anorexia is such a "middle-class white girl thing," and the therapist had been the head of mental services and had probably seen a lot of people with "much more serious problems," "really dying out there." Jeanne also recalled that her father had difficulties in understanding her disorder against the background of his own childhood as one of ten children in a poor family:

> He would tell us how meal times were just this huge battle of who could get the most food, because there was so little to go around. And he says, and he said that to me also when I wasn't eating, that he could never understand people who didn't want to eat. That he would always want to eat. It was this sort of leftover feeling for him, from when he was growing up, that eating was survival, whereas to me it was a way of becoming undesirable.

## *Taru*

When asked what she thought of theories on anorexia, Taru stated that she granted that her anorexia was related to "a need for approval." Yet, she was critical of descriptions of what was wrong with anorexics, saying they were too similar to the sports discourses that had fueled her anorexia:

> I am really sensitive to talk about women, about how women this and that. If you read sports or fitness magazines, it seems that all women are freaks of nature, all women are weak and bad and

everything else. . . . The stories on anorexia in the magazines are very similar—it's about how these women are weak because they cannot take the ideological pressure, or their parents were wrong or their mothers were weak. I would not want to think of myself as a victim. As if it was caused by my mother or my father or the culture around me. I feel that at that situation [anorexia] was the most logical solution to the fundamental problem of my hips and ankles. [TFL]

For fifteen years Taru had done everything she could, putting herself through an excruciating regime of exercise and living off boiled rice and Tabasco sauce in order to become "enduring, light, strong, and flawless." Against this background, she did not accept discourses on anorexia that, once again, defined her as being a weak, flawed woman. In addition to being critical of popular discourses on eating disorders, Taru was also critical of people's perceptions of anorexics in everyday life:

I think there are several ways that people think of anorexia. There is this stance, typical of young men, that, oh shit, that's sick, and don't tell me that you're one of them too. This is an aggressive stance, whereas there is also this kind of understanding attitude, typical of older women, who have sympathy or pity toward the anorexic and are, for example, careful not to offer her any food. . . . And then there are those who view anorexics as women who think they are too precious to eat, or that anorexia is a consequence of too high standards of living, that this is simply something these women have come up with. [TFL]

Taru was critical not only of "aggressive" views on anorexia, which view it as sick or ridiculous, but she also problematized an empathetic or pitying attitude toward women with eating disorders, because it infantilizes the anorexic in a motherly fashion. Just like Jeanne, Taru had identified the discourse on anorexics as defining them as rich or "precious" girls or "spoiled brats." Unlike Jeanne, who viewed it as indicating the privilege of anorexic women in comparison to people with more serious problems, Taru interpreted it as another way of stigmatizing and discounting women with eating disorders.

## *Eleanora*

In the interview, Eleanora stated that she found discourses on anorexia sometimes useful, but mostly she was not really interested in them. She thought some of the standard explanations, such as fear of growing up, were clichéd. Much like some of the women interviewed by Malson (1998) and Rich (2006), Eleanora could not really relate to the descriptions; she thought of them as superficial.

At one point in the research process, I sent a manuscript, based on some of my interviews, to the women for comments (see Saukko, 2000). Eleanora was the only one to get back to me. It took her a year to e-mail me, saying that it had been difficult for her to write to tell me that she did not agree with my depiction of her as the "poor, lonely child." She said it played into the general victimization of anorexics in that it reinforced the idea that anorexics are "weak" and did not acknowledge the fact that they can also be strong. She continued that she thought that having recovered from an ordeal, such as anorexia, was proof that these women were strong.

On a self-reflective note, Eleanora commented that even though she wanted to emphasize that anorexic women can be strong, she also wanted to acknowledge that the idea that women always have to be strong and independent may be counterproductive. At the time she wrote the e-mail, Jarmo was no longer part of Eleanora's life. Soon after graduating from the university she had been offered the job she had always aspired to: an entry-level position in an international organization, which promised to launch her into a global career. However, Eleanora had not accepted the position but had followed her new lover to Italy. She had a much less secure and less glamorous job in a nongovernmental organization. Eleanora wrote that her life decisions and life course had sidetracked her adamant career orientation and made her feel more free and happy. She also stated that she felt insecure about her future.

Eleanora's story provided a sad account of a childhood tragedy that rendered her feeling lonely and abandoned, looking for love and nurturance. However, Eleanora was not satisfied with my telling of this sad story. She felt my rendition framed her as a "poor victim" to be pitied and denied her strength and her dignity. Like Taru, Eleanora wanted to be acknowledged as having strength; she wanted to occupy the desirable position of a self-directing, strong subject who steers her life rather than being someone who is steered by outside forces.

However, Eleanora's story did not follow the same course as Taru's account. Similar to Taru, Eleanora emphasized that anorexic women are too often framed as weak and victimized. But Eleanora acknowledged that an "adamant" pursuit of strength and career has its drawbacks and suppresses other values and ways of life. At that point in her life, Eleanora had chosen a more traditional female path and followed a love to a foreign country; she noted that her decision had made her happier, but also left her feeling insecure. Eleanora was ambivalent about the discourse on female strength and success, acknowledging both its possibilities and its one-dimensionality. Her story illustrates the difficulties women face as they try to combine competitive careerism with living a fulfilling life and self-determination with relationships, and how discourses advocating simple strength are not particularly helpful for negotiating this space.

## Crystal

When asked how she thought bulimia was described in the public domain, Crystal said that bulimia was seen as "opposite of anorexia," with bulimics portrayed as "pretty out of control, on lots of levels, with their emotions, sex, and drugs, and food." She said that she fitted the descriptions "to the tee," seeing herself in the depictions of women who were "extroverted, a lot of stuff with the mother, things like that."

Crystal stated that bulimia was mostly about "psychological, emotional stuff," and she thought it was not so much a social issue. Thinking about the social dimension of bulimia, Crystal thought back to her interest in food politics and her therapist Lisa, noting that for her bulimia was not political, and that she did not want to get political about it either:

> I never got much of a political or feminist awareness [from bulimia]. It was always very humiliating or secretive, and I never really became a political activist. Not like Lisa—she took her things and questions out there and turned it into a political statement, made a career out of it. I don't think I will. For myself, the lesson is that food is not all that important. Taking it from the opposite perspective, there are so many other things more important than body shape or food, it's just too limited . . . too limiting.

Having become bulimic, partly as a consequence of her political interest in food, Crystal did not want to politicize her eating disorder. Her attitude to her beliefs about the importance of vegetarianism and its social and global ramifications was ambivalent; she did not deny their importance or rightfulness but she also did not want to return to trying to transform the world through her eating, drawing attention not only to the worldly but also to the obsessive and inward-directed nature of politicizing individual consumption and habits.

After recovering from bulimia, Crystal "sadly" became clinically depressed. "It sort of makes sense," she said, "because bingeing and purging had been my coping mechanism and you take those away and these terrible things start to happen." Crystal assessed her depression as much worse than bulimia. She recovered from it slowly with the aid of several therapists. One of the therapists did "character work" with her, which she found particularly helpful:

> You give the different people in yourself voices, and names and colors, and personalities. I've got eight of them. One of them is Larry; he is a 40–50 year-old-man, who's fat, on the couch, probably drinking beer, eating popcorn or something. He's a real downer, very cynical, ooh, very depressed. And his wife is Liz, and she is young, she's like in her 20s. And she's really energetic and bubbling and enthusiastic, and she is almost always on her bike, driving away into the distance. And these different people are having a yelling match, or just not talking to each other, but having these different agendas, but if you can give them voice and hash it out, you can begin to make them interact.

Character work helped Crystal to acknowledge and come to terms with her different personality traits, rather than suppressing the "loser" and "downer" element in her, as she had attempted to do through bulimic practices. The therapy in particular helped her give up the chase for the one-dimensional active, self-determining subject. This image—the self Crystal named Liz—reigned during Crystal's experience of bulimia. Such a self-determining subject is also posited as the ideal in many diagnostic discourses that try to make sense and treat eating disorders.

## *The Four Women*

The four women's reflections on discourses on eating disorders are varied and, on several occasions, contradict each other. Jeanne's account of feeling "stupid" for having had anorexia, which she viewed as "self-indulgent," contrasts with Taru's piercing critique of discourses on anorexia that frame anorexics as "weak," "victims," or "too precious to eat." For Jeanne, the idea that anorexics have succumbed to false consciousness was empowering; it made her realize that she had been guided by a reactionary and sexist ideology, and she felt stupid about it now. For Taru, the idea of anorexics falling victim to ideologies repeated the notions of women's weakness and vulnerability that she had found ubiquitous in sports discourses, which had originally fueled her starving. Jeanne and Taru are not right or wrong about the discourse on anorexics as victims of social influences, but their different accounts bring into relief the empowering and disempowering dimensions of this discourse.

Jeanne and Taru both have strong views about descriptions of women with eating disorders. Still, their words have echoes that invite other interpretations, illustrating the continuous interplay between voice and discourse. Jeanne's comments about feeling stupid for having anorexia tell that even she thought the descriptions of anorexia were "right," they also humiliated her. Taru's anger at being framed weak or as a victim not only tell about the problems with defining women as perpetually lacking in strength but also consolidate the dominance of the social ideal of strength, which makes us churn whenever we are accused of lacking it.

Jeanne's and Crystal's views about the political aspect of eating disorders are also interestingly contradictory. Jeanne locates her experience of starving firmly in the political context of the Reagan era's neoliberalism, which fueled her competitiveness. On the contrary, Crystal does not think of her bulimia as political, associating her bulimia with emotional issues that she was trying to "numb" with eating as well as her unusual eating habits. Jeanne's story brings to the fore how politicizing the personal can be empowering—how an individual can be motivated to political action through a personally meaningful experience. Crystal's story illustrates how claims about the political nature of a condition can be experienced as alienating—as if the words of the anorexic/bulimic woman are captured to make somebody else's political statement. On the other hand, Crystal's reluctance to politicize her bulimia relates to her negative experience of politicizing her eating, which highlights how aiming to effectuate political change through personal behavior can also be disempowering—how it can lead to an inward-directed struggle to control, and a subsequent loss of control, of one's behavior. While the political effectiveness or ineffectiveness of changing the world by individual choice has been amply debated, for example, in environmental politics, the alienating or damaging personal effects of attempts to politicize everyday behavior have rarely been discussed.

Jeanne's and Crystal's both similar and different experiences and interpretations of these experiences are also guided by different social regimes or logics. Jeanne's account follows a straightforward modern idea of emancipation: she sees herself as coming to a feminist consciousness after realizing that she has followed a politically and personally destructive ideology. Crystal had originally followed a more postmodern or New Age sensibility according to which "if you change your perception you change the experience of your body and your world" (Chopra 1993, p. 6). This sensibility is geared towards effectuating micro-changes with the intent of setting in motion systemic changes in the macro-environment. This component of these two stories—the different associations between politics and eating disorders—is similar to the different ideals of autonomous and flexible self discussed in the context of media coverage of Karen Carpenter and Princess Diana. As such, they further illustrate how timely sensibilities seep into individuals' self-understandings and actions, where they acquire new local meanings and have contradictory implications.

Regardless of how they differ, the women's accounts reveal a shared ambivalence towards discourses. For example, Eleanora, similar to Taru, does not want to be described as a weak victim, but, similar to Jeanne, she is also critical of the discourse on strength or the "superwoman." She acknowledges the promises and problems embedded in being a strong, competitive individual and in taking a softer, less adamant, and more relational stance. Eleanora's life situation, which had positioned her to view these two paths with some clarity, was not easy. Yet, her comments illustrate a critically self-reflective stance through which she evaluates the different sides of social ideals rather than stubbornly pursues one. Crystal's discussion of character work, which had allowed her to appreciate different sides of her personality, illustrates a similar reflective life philosophy. Taru and Jeanne are both also critical of discourses, with their criticisms focused on one angle of the discourse on strength.

The methodology used in the interviews invited critical self-reflection. Yet, it is fair to say that in their accounts, the women tell about a life philosophy that critically interrogates all subject positions offered by various social institutions and sensibilities. The methodology and the women's views work in tandem, so that the analytical approach allows the women's philosophy to come through and helps to bring it into sharper conceptual relief.

## *Both/And*

In her classic article on alternative notions of validity of research, Lather (1993) identifies ironic, paralogic, and situated validities. Lather envisions that under the new rules of validity the legitimation of research would not depend on its closeness to "truth" but on its ability to "unjam" closed truths of the past (p. 676). The new criteria for validity values research that sets old truths into motion by presenting multiple interpretations and representations of its object of study, leaving different explanations and views in tension and foregrounding the views of the silenced and the subaltern.

The other sources that I have drawn from here, Ronai (1998), Bakhtin (1981) and Denzin (2002), share Lather's aim to subvert established truths and present silenced experiences in a manner that permanently holds them in suspense by drawing attention to their always represented nature. My aim has been to destabilize established truths about the anorexic self by drawing attention to their constructed, limited, and limiting nature. However, my intention is not to simply deconstruct the concept of the anorexic self, but, in a more constructive spirit, to render it multidimensional.

The trouble with much research on lived experience of eating disorders is that it is grounded on a normative either/or logic, categorizing statements, states of mind, and societies as *either* pathological *or* healthy, *either* oppressive *or* emancipatory. Trying to make sense of and learning from the interviews I conducted, I have sought to employ a research approach grounded on a both/and logic. This approach helps in exploring how discourses on the anorexic as a victim of harmful social influences or ideologies can be *both* feminist or empowering *and* sexist and denigrating. It also allows us to see how discourses on the anorexic as a privileged, white, middle-class girl can draw critical attention to aspects of middle-class culture that fuel eating disorders *and* highlight the relative privilege of many women with eating disorders in comparison to the poor and ethnic minorities. Further, it allows us to see that these discourses also articulate a sexist disdain towards whining spoiled brats who think they are too precious to eat. Similarly, it facilitates a more nuanced analysis of discourses that encourage women to be strong and successful. These discourses can: inspire women to get ahead in a male-dominated world; be founded on naïve individualist voluntarism, which glosses over the structural impediments that make it excessively difficult for women to succeed and instead blames women's personal or gendered qualities for failure; *and* suppress other values, such as relationality, and notions of a fulfilling life that fall out of the ambit of competitive individualism. An analytical approach sensitive to multiple dimensions of discourses and experiences also helps us comprehend how politicizing eating behaviors can foster a personally healing and politically active feminist or globally oriented consciousness. The approach can simultaneously acknowledge that politicizing eating or eating disorders can seem alienating or lead to the implosion of politics into an obsessive regulation of minute details of everyday life.

With hindsight, the women interviewed had learned to appreciate the multifaceted nature of discourses that invite us to be who we want to be, and contrasting the individual women's stories and self-reflections brings the multidimensionality of discourses on eating disorders into even clearer light. I contend that research, like the women, needs to acknowledge the complexity of discourses surrounding eating disorders. Researchers must develop modes of study that take this complexity into account if they are to work against the cultural logics that fuel the conditions.

# 6

# *From Time-Based Diagnosis to Space-Based Critical Reflection*

As seen in the previous chapter, anorexia frequently articulates a pursuit of a new self and body that would surpass the inadequacies a woman perceives plague her. At the same time, psychiatric, social scientific, and popular discourses mobilize anorexia to narrate powerful stories about psychological pathologies or inadequacies that blight individual anorexic women and political and social pathologies that afflict entire societies where anorexia breeds. These discourses also call for re-creating new feminine selves and bodies and better societies. It does not come as a surprise that the inadequacies the anorexic identifies in herself, and the inadequacies that clinical and social commentators identify in the anorexic and in the societies where it prevails, are strikingly alike, often affirming similar, historical normative notions about free or flexible self and society.

The problem with discussions on anorexia is that they implode, as noted by Probyn, the multiple meanings surrounding eating disorders into "one causal and moral discourse" (Probyn, 1987, p. 203). Thus the main shortcoming in these discussions is not necessarily their content but their form. As we've seen, discourses on anorexia frequently make distinctions between good and bad, healthy and misguided ways of being; the discourses fall into the same trap of dichotomous thinking as the anorexic does.

In this final chapter I will outline a methodological approach to studying anorexia differently. Most research on anorexia follows a time-oriented logic. It conceptualizes consciousness in terms of health and authenticity in contrast with pathology and inauthenticity. This line of inquiry tends to view the social or political agendas that anorexia articulates in monolithic and often abstract terms, such as "sexism." It ends up conceiving the relationship between the self and society in opposition to each other and proposes a linear, time-based development whereby the anorexic matures or graduates into an independent, true, or healthy selfhood. This true self usually articulates the dominant cultural values about self and society that inform eating disorders in the first place.

Space-based analysis conceptualizes consciousness in terms of multiple voices that coexist, converse, and come into conflict side by side as if in space, rather than in hierarchic time. Such a conception invites us to be free and together, maintain our ground and be adaptable, be feminine and masculine, and so on (Hermans & Kempen, 1993). It views politics not as a system but as a complex social struggle between different actors and agendas that produces contradictory cultural formations, such as the current idealization of thinness and the diagnostic discourse on anorexia (Jasanoff, 2004; Marcus, 1998). This analytical framework explores the relationship between the self and society in terms of resonances between the intrapersonal space of contradictory polyvocal conversations and the political space of social struggles between varied agendas and groups (Volosinov, 1973).

Rather than denounce or celebrate certain discursive positions, a spatially oriented approach helps to unpack the contradictory personal and political implications of ideals, such as thinness or autonomy, that inform an anorexic's starving or her treatment. As such it cultivates a less anorexic or simplistically judgmental and more open, critically self-reflective way of relating to our selves, others, and the societies in which we live.

In what follows I will outline how to make sense of the personal and political implications of both discourses that inform and discourses that diagnose eating disorders using a space-based heuristic. I will also discuss why this methodological approach is particularly useful for understanding eating disorders.

## *Narrative Therapy and the Discursive Self*

As observed by Hoskins and Leseho (1996, also Henriques et al., 1984), the metaphors that counsellors use to describe the nature and character of the self influence their therapeutic practice. Much psychiatric theorizing on anorexia is informed by what Hoskins and Leseho would call a "unitary" understanding of self, which perceives that a core "true self" exists and which views therapy as helping clients to "discard aspects of the self that do not relate to the true self" (p. 244). This model usually posits the social world as a possible source of contamination that hinders the true or autonomous self from emerging. This is exemplified by, for example, Hilde Bruch's theories and practice as discussed in chapter 3.

Narrative therapy is grounded on an understanding of the self not as something essential to be discovered but as "in a continual process of becoming" (Hoskins & Leseho, 1996, p. 245). This means that narrative therapy does not adhere to the classical psychological notion of a stable, unitary self but views the self as being constituted by social narratives or discourses in interaction with significant others, the media, and other social institutions that disseminate and re-create social and cultural norms for thinking and behaving. Due to the constructed and fluid nature of the self, the self is seen as continuously transforming as the form and content of interaction around it change. As a consequence, the aim of narrative therapy is not to help the client discover her true self but to support her in "renarrating" a different self. One of the techniques used to facilitate a narrative reconstruction of the self is a process that White and Epston (1990) have termed "externalization."

White and Epston (1990, p. 38) define externalization as "an approach to therapy that encourages persons to objectify and, at times, to personify the problem that they experience as oppressive." In *Biting the Hand That Starves You*, a book on one narrative approach to anorexia and bulimia, Maisel, Epston, and Borden describe this externalization as delineating the "voice of anorexia/bulimia," which refers to "the meanings that support and strengthen its regime" (2004, p. 21). Examples of meanings that support eating disorders that Maisel, Epston, and Borden mention include feelings of guilt, inferiority, and badness and cultures and contexts that emphasize achievement, competition, thinness, perfection, and self-sacrifice.

Maisel, Epston, and Borden's approach to anorexia is laudable because they do not locate the problem of anorexia in the woman's self, which is traditionally viewed as weak or overly permeable to outside discourses, but in the social discourses that constitute our subjectivities. Their aim is to develop a technique that helps the woman to gain critical distance from the social narratives that have constituted her self, and as such the approach comes close to Foucault's idea of a technology of the self (Foucault, 1982), which precisely encourages critical interrogation of the discourses that have shaped us. However, on closer inspection it remains an open question whether, or to what extent, the attempt to silence the anorexic voice is different from the classical pursuit of a unitary or true self.

Gremillion (2003) has addressed this question and defends the narrative therapeutic approach against criticisms that the therapeutic paradigm "romanticizes healthy identities as Other to anorexia" (p. 196). Gremillion argues that the process of externalizing does not aim to "kill off" problems but to situate them outside of the person, so that their "histories, contexts and effects" can be explored (p. 203). To exemplify her point, Gremillion discusses Johnella Bird's description of a narrative therapy session with a man who had been caught intruding on people's property while looking through windows at women (pp. 201–203). She notes how the therapist asks the man, "What sort of look would you be using?" for women, which locates the source of the problem in a culturally defined way of leering at women rather than in the man himself, in which case the therapist could have asked him, "How would you be looking at women?" Rather than aiming to suppress the bad peeping self, narrative therapy can be understood to question the premises of a socially constructed way of looking at women. The strength of the narrative therapeutic approach in this case is that it brings into relief and problematizes the customary male, social violence lodged in the practice of looking. I would argue its shortcoming is that it takes a fairly one-dimensional attitude toward this socially defined way of looking and does not address the pleasures embedded in gazing at female bodies. It also does not address its own complicity with social policing, as it bypasses the complex politics that regulates how the male gaze can be applied in a way that is socially acceptable, which clearly does not include intruding onto properties and peering through windows.

In a similar vein, narrative therapy's critical assessment of discourses that promote anorexia sometimes end up rather flat. For example, in *Biting the Hand That Starves You*, Maisel, Epston, and Borden (2004) extensively discuss perfectionism as one of the typical manifestations of the anorexic/bulimic or "a/b" voice. They discuss how the a/b voice sets impossibly high standards. It demands the woman be "the best" and asserts that "if another person's performance exceeds your own, you have failed to attain perfection," which "inevitably result[s] in confirmation of failures and deficiencies" (p. 36). They go on to discuss the story of Amy, who learned to speak back to the a/b voice of perfectionism. Rather than rushing to aqua aerobics in the morning, Amy had "taken her own pleasure" and stayed in bed. She slowly learned to differentiate between her own preferred lifestyle and anorexia's lifestyle and imagined the two in terms of binaries: "walking versus forced marching, doing things because you want to versus doing things because you have to, freedom versus imprisonment" (p. 194) and anorexic "rituals" versus anti-anorexic "creativity" (p. 202).

For Amy, breaking the spell of a torturous, picture-perfect performance by positing it as an outside force or voice was useful. It allowed her to gain critical distance from the social discourses that guided her to live a painful life. However, the way in which Maisel, Epston, and Borden discuss perfectionism has two, interrelated problematic features. First, their discussion is relatively depoliticized (also Hepworth, 1999). Second, they create a dichotomy between anorexic ritualistic and forced perfectionism and a kind of anti-anorexic creative learning to take it easy. These two shortcomings reproduce the classical psychological professional perspective that may allude to social influences but envisions change in terms of changing an individual's attitudes and behavior. Furthermore, the contrast between an a/b voice and its alternatives resembles the traditional juxtaposition between a socially defined artificial and pathological self and a genuine, self-defined healthy self, even if it acknowledges that also healthy selves are socially shaped. As such, this line of therapy does not discuss the structural aspects of perfectionism or the different sides of the discourse on perfectionism or its alternative, the "preferred" discourse promoting a more relaxed lifestyle.

Maisel, Epston, and Borden acknowledge that perfectionism breeds in certain institutional contexts, such as competitive sports and academia, but they bypass this observation quickly. They make little of the structural factors that demand perfectionism, wherein as the levels of educational attainment rise, inhuman performance becomes the norm—particularly for middle-class girls, if they want to meet the expectations of their parents, schools, and the professional job market (Walkerdine, Lucey, & Melody, 2001). Furthermore, comparative competitiveness, the idea of separating the wheat from chaff, is also becoming an increasingly integral part of contemporary neoliberal governments' policies. Consider the new examination procedures, which fuel all kinds of anxieties, including eating disorders, in schools (Evans, Rich, & Holroyd, 2004). Being silent about these structural factors makes it seem as if the anorexic is being a perfectionist because she is misguided by cultural discourses. This does not acknowledge the deep rationality of perfectionism in the current social context; it does not acknowledge that perfectionism is the only available strategy for attaining success for many women, who are pushed to extreme trying by the structural imperative, sugarcoated by the ideology of equal opportunities, that tells women and blacks that they can succeed as well as white men if they just try hard enough. As such, narrative therapy does not capture the empowering aspect of perfectionism and success, which makes it appealing to young women in the first place. Maisel, Epston, and Borden also rather naïvely posit that overcoming perfectionism in the lives of young women is a matter of telling a different story rather than addressing deeply ingrained processes that maintain inequality through measurement of performance.

Constructing a polarized opposition between perfectionism as the externalized enemy and a "kick back and relax" attitude as the preferred lifestyle also obscures the ambivalence of the alternative. The suggestions that we should learn to relax or downsize in the name of enjoying the pleasures of living and doing something creative and worthwhile rather than pursuing the monotonous or ritualistic rat race is very much a dominant trope in current British and American popular imagination. While this new trope may challenge the tooth-and-nail competitive culture, it is silent about the fact that the alternative lifestyle of teaching yoga and taking time to smell the roses is attainable only by a privileged few. On a more general level, this attitude may also buttress the "flexibility" ideal, discussed in relation to media discourses on Princess Diana in chapter 4, which legitimizes new, often exploitative feminized, part-time, and temporary labor patterns by framing them as promoting self-actualization.

## *From One Voice to Many*

My critique of the narrative therapeutic approach represented by Maisel, Epston, and Borden does not mean that I consider the paradigm worthless. The notion of a discursively constructed self and the idea that psychology should be reconfigured as a practice whereby individuals can gain critical insight into the social discourses that shape their identities and actions is a fruitful one. However, White and Epston's (1990) and Maisel, Epston, and Borden's (2004) practice of constructing an enemy voice, such as the a/b voice, tends to reproduce the dichotomous distinction between good and bad self that underpins the anorexic's practice of starving and most scholarly and therapeutic approaches to it.

A narrative therapeutic approach developed by Hermans and Kempen (1993), which views discourses in polyvocal rather than dichotomous terms, offers a useful complement to Maisel, Epston, and Borden's work. Drawing on Bakhtin, Hermans and Kempen state that much narrative analysis is time-oriented, as in classical narrative writing that proceeds from a beginning, through a middle, to an end, or in therapy that strives for a synthesis between different selves or silencing of a particular aspect of the self. On the contrary, Hermans and Kempen suggest thinking about narrative in spatial terms, which allows for viewing "all things as being coexistent and to perceive and depict things side by side and simultaneously, as if in space rather than time" (p. 42). A spatial way of thinking about voices that speak through experience allows for coexistence, and dialogues and conflicts between the voices, avoiding the problem embedded with Epston and White's formulation of externalization, where one voice is framed as the villain to be suppressed.

Hermans and Kempen (1993, pp. 81–88) give an example of polyvocal therapy in discussing the case of Alice, who identified two sides or characters in her personality: an open and a closed one. Originally Alice considered her "open" or extroverted, cheerful, and helping side as more dominant and positive and considered her closed side, which preferred being alone and maintaining boundaries, as less prominent and negative. However, during the narrative evaluation Alice began to acknowledge her closed character and to value it more positively. She began to say no to people who wanted her company or help. Hermans and Kempen conclude that the example of Alice demonstrates that the self is a dynamic entity, which evolves as different characters are pushed to the front or the back in various life situations or in therapy. Furthermore, the example also illustrates the presence of a different order self, which is aware of the various subselves and their relationships (p. 92). Hermans and Kempen suggest imagining this higher order self as a "composer"; it does not synthetize the various characters or voices into seamless harmony but assembles them together so each can illuminate the other's advantages and disadvantages.

If one compares Maisel, Epston, and Borden's (2004) analysis of Amy and Hermans and Kempen's (1993) analysis of Alice, the similarities and differences between these two narrative approaches come to light. Maisel, Epston, and Borden encourage the client to speak against the voice of anorexia and perfectionism, running the risk of juxtaposing perfectionism and antiperfectionism. Hermans and Kempen encourage the client to explore different voices and to leave them in tension with one another. This approach allows the client to explore the both enabling and positive and disabling and negative sides of various voices or characters, which may embrace being open, closed, a perfectionist/overachiever, or relaxed. The strength of both approaches is their ability to open a discursive position (such as being perfect or open) up for critical reflection and to introduce alternative ways of looking at one's self and the world. However, Hermans and Kempen's approach better helps to maintain a critically reflective attitude towards all discursive positions. The anorexic experience is often driven by a desire to create a "new," better self (such as beautiful high-achiever, perfect ballet dancer, lovable beautiful woman, or altruistic vegetarian, to give examples from the interviews discussed in chapter 5), as well as to destroy an unacceptable self (e.g., Malson, 1998). The polyvocal narrative approach may enable the anorexic to critically examine the premises of her "new" self while also allowing her to acknowledge some of the good within or rationality of this self-project and to keep an equally open, critically reflective mind towards any alternatives.

Hermans and Kempen's notion of applying a spatial concept of the self is illuminative, as many discourses on eating disorders are informed by a time-based imagination. The time-based imagination conceives of a deep, internal self slowly finding itself through peeling off superficial social influences. The image reinforces a strict evaluative distinction between inner truth and outer falsity and, unsurprisingly, superficiality and artificiality are often associated with femininity, whereas deep, authentic internality is imagined as masculine (Malson, 1998, p. 157). Hermans and Kempen's spatial metaphor flattens out the topography, inviting contrasts and comparisons between different voices in a manner that does not compartmentalize them into enemies and friends but holds them in tension, illuminating their different, both harmful and enabling, dimensions.

## *Heterogeneous Politics*

While the narrative therapeutic ideas about the polyvocal nature of the voices that speak through the anorexic experience are helpful, they leave open the question of how to evaluate the empowering and disempowering effects of the various discursive positions circulating in the intrapersonal universe. Hermans and Kempen's discussion of narratives, such as being open or closed, come closer to outlining psychological character traits than social discourses, and their evaluation of the effects of the problems and possibilities of each position verges on a pluralistic or even relativistic acknowledgment that each position has two sides to it. The main achievement of critical research on anorexia has been to politicize the condition, calling close attention to the ways in which the discourses that inform women's starving (Bordo, 1993) and their treatment (Gremillion, 2003) have their origins in specific social and political agendas and contexts.

Oftentimes the political nature of anorexia is discussed at an abstract, allegorical level (see Clifford, 1986). It is argued, for example, that women's starving tells about the destructive effects of Western culture (Bordo, 1993), modernity (Giddens, 1991), or postmodernity (Spitzack, 1993). More detailed analyses have argued that anorexia bears witness to a social transition, wherein the woman's role is changing from being subservient and dependent towards becoming more independent (Bruch, 1978). In this situation the anorexic's starving articulates a woman's agony with contradictory demands; the woman aims to resolve the contradictory demands by attaining a thin body, which signifies both strength and self-determination and frailty and traditional feminine attractiveness (Bordo, 1993; Orbach, 1986). Gremillion (2003) has pointed out that therapeutic discourses on anorexia end up trying to resolve the historical, gendered dilemma by prescribing for anorexics the same social medicine, fitness and self-determination, that women with eating disorders are already self-administering at dangerous levels.

These studies illuminate how eating disorders and their diagnosis embody—and rupture within—certain broad cultural or epistemic sensibilities that shape the way in which we make sense of and act in the world (Foucault, 1973). While these observations are insightful, the problem with them is that they view discourses surrounding anorexia as too straightforwardly dominant. They tend to envision, either explicitly or implicitly, a utopian, temporal development from a sexist past toward an imaginary free future. In the imaginary future women have graduated into independence (Orbach, 1986) or developed a new, more female-orientated mode of being (Bordo, 1993) and therapeutic practices no longer prescribe for anorexic women more fitness but help them to "talk back" to the a/b voice and to adopt an anti-fitness, anti-anorexic, and more relaxed lifestyle (Gremillion, 2003; Maisel, Epston, & Borden, 2004).

Studies conducted within these critical frameworks have drawn attention to important broad social trends, inequalities, and domination. However, they tend to oversimplify the issue. They say little about what specific historical social struggles inform women's starving or the way in which we make sense of their starving. The broad political and theoretical pronouncements may also become counterproductive in that they become forgetful of their own downside. They are oblivious of the sexism embedded in definitions of anorexics as simple victims of mass or consumer culture or the fact that the "anti-anorexic" withdrawing from the rat race has become a dominant individualist fantasy in contemporary culture that does little to address the structural issues behind fitness/competitiveness or benefits of success—particularly for poor women and people of color, who have rarely tasted its fruits.

Science and technology studies (STS) offers a model for investigating the interaction between institutions (science, psychiatry), technologies (dieting, therapy), and society that is more nuanced than thinking in terms of broad trends. The paradigm understands these interactions in terms of mutual "co-production," where neither technologies or institutions nor society is given primacy. This avoids the excesses of both technological determinism and social constructivism (Jasanoff, 2004). Studies using the STS framework differ in terms of whether they emphasize the smooth congruence between institutions, technologies, and social regimes or the disjunctures between them. For example, Petersen and Bunton (2002) note that testing for genetic predispositions to disease with a view to encouraging people to change their lifestyle fits like a glove with the current neoliberal zeitgeist underlining self-responsibility. Somewhat differently, Hilgartner (2004) has observed that efforts to render genomic data manageable brought about a new form of collective property ownership in terms of DNA reference libraries, as discussed in Hilgartner's detailed ethnographic and historical study. Petersen and Bunton emphasize the tight connection between genetic technologies and contemporary zeitgeist, just like Bordo (1993) and Gremillion (2003) emphasize the closeness of contemporary ideologies about individual fitness and the experience and treatment of anorexia. Again somewhat differently, Hilgartner examines a surprising, even if contradictory, development of collective property in science against the backdrop of individualistic and competitive social values and laboratory life.

My argument—that the notions of autonomous or flexible self, which often inform both anorexic women's starving and their treatment, are deeply embedded in the postwar and 1990s social and political context—seems to support the idea that there is a close connection between social regimes and technologies of the self. However, this is only part of the truth. When this notion is investigated in more detail, as I have done in chapter 3, it becomes apparent that the ideal autonomous self is a more complicated animal. In postwar scientific and popular understandings, the obese and the anorexic both suffered from a nonautonomous self in relation to consumer culture, succumbing to overconsuming either tempting mass-produced foods or images (of thin models) (also Schwartz, 1986, Stearns, 1997). The critiques of consumer culture, however, were shot through with contradictory agendas. They frequently articulated old middle-class or intellectualist disdain towards people of lower social class or different ethnicity (such as Bruch's Eastern European immigrant children) as well as the newly affluent suburbanites. Criticism against consumer culture were leveled by the left-wing Frankfurt school, which interpreted it as opium of the masses, but mass culture also fueled anticommunist paranoias and laments about the loss of rugged American individualism. Criticisms of postwar suburban domesticity, associated with mass culture and nonautonomous subservience, could also articulate both feminist concerns and sexist disregard of women. Thus, rather than being either emancipatory or oppressive, the ideal of autonomy in relation to eating disorders turns out to be complicated, articulating many diverse and contradictory social agendas and developments.

Understanding the political nature of discourses in terms of being co-produced by a wide array of actors, things, technologies, and social developments helps us to both appreciate unities that exist between social regimes and cultural ideals/technologies and to pay attention to the messiness of the process. Exploring the messiness of the players co-producing the discourse on autonomy helps us to make sense of the contradictions, rather than a simple sexist false consciousness, characterizing the anorexic's experience of starving. Similarly, it helps us make sense of the contradictory, both humiliating and healing, feelings women have about being diagnosed anorexic.

Science and technology studies helps to highlight that personal thoughts and behaviors are shaped by social processes and structures and that changing them requires getting political about these processes rather than merely changing thoughts and meanings (which narrative therapy is often oblivious of). It helps to understand the social processes in a manner that draws attention to their many facets and contradictions and calls for more nuanced feminist engagement with political issues, such as the alleged deleterious effects of mass culture or fitness, associated with eating disorders. Paying attention to the complexity of the political processes is particularly important when investigating the politics behind women's starving and its treatment, as dichotomous notions of healthy and pathological society and self are the problem underpinning eating disorders and addressing this problem requires more subtle modes of both political and psychological analysis.

Marcus's idea (1998) of multi-sited ethnography offers a useful heuristic and practical tool with which to make sense of the complex co-production of discursive formations that is grounded in spatial metaphors. Marcus has criticized anthropology for its tendency to understand the relationship between local cultures and global cultures as a system imposing itself on a lifeworld (which is similar to understanding anorexics as falling victims to sexist society). He has argued for studying how cultural and social formations "form across and within multiple sites of activity" (Marcus, 1998, p. 80). "System" in multi-sited ethnography is not a presupposed monolith but is viewed as emerging from interactions and flows (of ideas, people, technologies, and things) between different sites (also Appadurai, 1997).

Marcus identifies two ways of doing multi-sited ethnography. The first, "strategic" mode, studies only one site but maps how what is happening in the location is linked, through the flows of people, ideas, money, and things (see Appadurai, 1997), with what is going on in other sites. In this book I have strategically studied a single site, such as Bruch's work, and mapped its connections to other sites and spheres of life—such as immigration policy, Cold War international and national politics, developments in American psychiatry and feminism—all mediated through the flow of ideas (often in the form of intertextual citations), people (such as Bruch's movement from Nazi Germany to the United States or her connection with Frieda Fromm-Reichmann), institutions and technologies (psychoanalysis), and so on. The second strategy is to "follow" the research object across multiple sites, exploring how it changes as it gets associated with different issues in different contexts. I have also "followed" anorexia across multiple sites, such as history of psychiatry, news media, and personal contexts of various women, which has revealed different ways of defining anorexia that are associated with diverse politics.

Marcus's heuristic helps to map the social agendas, actors, and processes that co-produce discourses on anorexia at various historical times and in diverse social places. This methodology allows us to examine the messy, multi-(f)actorial shaping of a discursive formation as if in space rather than interpreting anorexia against a broad predefined discursive formation, such as modernity, in time.

## *Between Personal and Political*

Multi-sited ethnography's view of politics as taking shape within and between different sites in space is in good synchrony with narrative therapy's idea of consciousness as constituted by different social voices as if in space. Volosinov's (1973) "sociological" theory of consciousness helps to connect the two.

Volosinov argues that consciousness "takes shape and being in the material of signs created by an organized group in the process of its social intercourse" (Volosinov, 1973, p. 13). What this means is that voices or discourses that speak in an individual's consciousness stem from the life experience and agenda of a specific social group and that, as a consequence, at any given time there will be many social discourses that collude and coalesce with each other. By tracing intrapersonal discourses to social groups and agendas located at a specific time and place, dialogic theory helps to unpack the nexus between personal experience and the political sphere. As such, Volosinov's theory helps to conceptualize a spatial way of analyzing the personal and the political and their relationship in terms of exploring connections between intrapersonal contestations and contradictions and social struggles between different social groups, constituencies and agendas. His framework suggests examining how the social contradictions characterizing the discourses that fuel and diagnose eating disorders are translated into and negotiated through contests between intrapersonal voices in the anorexic's consciousness.

To think through what this means, let me turn back to Jeanne's story discussed in chapter 5. Looking back to her experience of anorexia as an undergraduate student, Jeanne interpreted her starving as "symptomatic of the Reagan years" when "women were supposed to have it all and be extremely successful in all realms." Although Jeanne thought that anorexia taught her an important lesson that she can be "vulnerable to cultural messages," she also described that she felt "uncomfortable" and "stupid" about having had the condition. Interpreted conventionally, Jeanne's story comes across as a classic temporal account of coming out of false consciousness, which resembles the "restoration" narrative, ubiquitous in biomedical sciences (Frank, 1995). Reading Jeanne's story using the spatial heuristic of juxtaposing voices rather than categorizing them as true or false brings into relief two intrapersonal voices, speaking both about political critique and self-shame, which bears witness to the empowering and disempowering accents of her self-interpretation. Connecting these two contradictory voices to social struggles helps us to understand how Jeanne's tension-riddled personal narrative articulates beguiling social struggles. Her critique of herself as succumbing to an individualist and sexist conservative ideology resonates with an American left-liberal social discourse critical of the ideologies of personal responsibility and entrepreneurship that have characterized the recent U.S. neoconservative governments from Reagan to George W. Bush. However, at the same time, Jeanne's shame or discomfort about having "stupidly" become anorexic tell about the double-edged nature of the American left-wing agenda, which since the postwar mass-culture critiques have articulated a sexist and intellectualist disdain for women and the lower middle-classes associated with psychological regression and reactionary politics.

Fleshing out the multiple accents in Jeanne's intrapersonal story and mapping them onto contradictory social struggles enables a nuanced analysis of the complex tensions structuring the lived and social worlds where anorexia happens. My argument in this book is that the traditional diagnostic way of defining the anorexic's self as lacking in terms of a specific cultural norm, such as autonomy or flexibility, fosters the anorexic mentality of adamant pursuit of a dominant social norm. The mode of inquiry informed by the heuristics of space allows for a more dialogic and self-reflective exploring of the contradictory personal implications and political investments of these norms. This does not mean resorting to relativism, as acknowledging that a social norm is not *either* emancipatory *or* oppressive but can often be *both* empowering *and* disempowering at the same time is not relativistic in any sense. It rather admits that discourses have more than one side to them, and all sides need to be tackled if we are to achieve sustainable personal peace or political progress.

## *Coming Full Circle*

This book has its origins in my anger or frustration with discourses on anorexia, which I felt described women with eating disorders in a way that was not only denigrating but also counterproductive. Having spent many years analyzing discourses on anorexia, and their personal implications and their political agendas in detail, I have reassessed my original reaction. While being angry about injustices and unfairness is necessary—and the chapters of this book contain my angry remarks about understandings of anorexia—it also blinds.

Analyses of anorexia are often filled with anger about images of thinness and treatment of women. However, unreflective denouncements in this area have produced problematic normative understandings about what is pathological about the anorexic self and the society in which we live. I have tried to draw myself close to the raw feelings that I and others have about eating disorders as well as distance myself from these feelings, and I have sought to look at the issue also from other perspectives to see whether they would reveal different angles, social programs, or feelings at play.

The theories and methodologies used throughout this book, such as Hermans and Kempen's (1993) narrative therapy, Volosinov's (1973) polyvocal notion of consciousness, Foucault's (1984) genealogy, Ronai's (1998) layered account, Richardson's (2000) understanding of methods and writing as prisms, and Marcus's (1998) multi-sited ethnography all articulate multiperspectival modes of inquiry. Deleuze and Guattari's (1987) discussion of research as "quilting" nicely encapsulates the ideas expressed in this body of work. Deleuze and Guattari distinguish modes of doing research that follow either the logic of an "embroidered" quilt or the logic of a "patchwork" quilt. Embroidered quilts have a center, and they develop a continuous pattern throughout the work. Traditional social scientific research, which traces a pattern, such as the cause of eating disorders, across research material, is a technique analogous to that of making an embroidered quilt. On the contrary, patchwork quilts have no center, and the basic motif (the patch) is multiple, giving rise to more rhythmic resonances and disjunctures that account for the unity of and tensions within the piece (p. 476).

The overall aim of Deleuze and Guattari's (1987) oeuvre is to unjam customary ways of doing research and approaching issues (with special reference to psychoanalysis). They seek to establish "lines of flight" that shatter established "assemblages." These "lines of flight" are practices or escape routes that challenge the "assemblages" that bring order to social reality through thinking and actions based on linear and dichotomous notions of causality (such as notions of the anorexic who falls ill due to overconsumption of images or due to lack of personal flexibility). Deleuze and Guattari's notion of "rhythmic resonances" helps to view the relationship between the self and society not in terms of cause and effect but more as tenuous vibrations. Similarly, it helps us to understand social formations and personal patterns of thought and behavior not as either free or compromised but as consisting of heterogeneous and unstable elements that have come together to form a specific psychological or political constellation or assemblage.

This way of thinking helps to open up the discourse on anorexia to new, alternative connections and explanations that come to light as connections pointing to different directions (rather than just one) come to light. At the same time, it also reveals the limiting or truncating effects of customary conceptions that always reroute anorexia to predictable grand narratives without being aware of the violent underside of these explanations (while remembering that they can be empowering as well, because they are multidimensional). Overall, the modes of doing research offered by Deleuze and Guattari, and the other authors cited in this book, invite us to continuously interrogate all discourses that suggest to us what we should be or what the world should be. This does not refer to a nihilistic, depressing skepticism but to a positive, productive ability to see that our personal lives and politics are more complex than they seem and therefore require more complex therapeutic and political strategies.

Thirty years after recovering from anorexia and many years after initiating this study, my original anger with discourses on eating disorders has nearly melted. It may have to do with my age; being 40-something and having been a mother and a professional academic for 10 years, I may have gotten used to occasional insults and life's disappointments and successes to the extent that I no longer feel the anger of my youth. However, the multi-perspectival research approach that I have taken has also led me to believe in a more measured, yet critical, habit of trying to make sense of personal and political life from different angles. I think such an approach to eating disorders offers a more balanced and nuanced—even if not easier—way of beginning to solve the personal dilemmas and political problems that the conditions articulate.

# Notes

## 3. Fat Boys and Goody Girls

1. Hilde Bruch's papers are archived in the McGovern Historical Research Center, Texas Medical Center Library, Houston Academy of Medicine, Houston, Texas (they are hereafter referred to as the Papers of Hilde Bruch). I would like to thank Margaret Irwin, JoAnn Pospisil, and Beth White for their kind help at the archive and the Graduate College of the University of Illinois, Urbana-Champaign, for a dissertation travel grant that enabled me to visit Houston.

2. If found this ad in Bruch's files. Bruch collected media articles and ads on obesity and anorexia throughout her career, and her clippings illuminate the changing popular perceptions of obesity and anorexia between 1930 and 1970 (see the Papers of Hilde Bruch, Series VII, Box 9, Folder 301, "Obesity clippings 1939–53").

3. The extent to which the notion of obesity is imposed on these children becomes evident in Bruch's remarks and notes about how the mothers did not consider their children to be obese, just "big." Although some of the mothers got worried about the prospect of their children not being normal, their lack of concern is manifested by the fact that they often missed appointments with the research group and did not obey the diets prescribed (see Bruch & Touraine, 1940).

4. "Obese Children notes, 1939–40," Series VIII, Box 11, Folders 359–369, the Papers of Hilde Bruch.

5. These observations are based on a more focused study of 40 obese children and their families. This study included, for example, visits to the children's homes. The results of this study were reported for the first time in Bruch & Touraine, 1940.

6. The environmental theory of mental illness gave more hope and, perhaps, better treatment to patients; yet it also contributed to the trend away from public asylums to private and thus elitist outpatient care, of which Bruch's practice is an example.

7. Bruch begins to focus on anorexia from the late fifties on, gradually treating fewer and fewer numbers of obese patients.

8. Bruch also used the then-popular Freudian notions of orality, Piaget's (1954) theory of development, and Bateson's famous idea of the "double bind" (Bateson et al., 1957) to argue for her theory.

9. Stated in Bruch's letter to Judy Folkenberg, a writer with the National Institute of Mental Health who was working on an article on anorexia, July 15, 1981, the Papers of Hilde Bruch, Series V, Box 6, Folder 189.

# References

Adorno, T., & Horkheimer, M. (1979). *Dialectic of enlightenment.* London: Verso.

American Psychiatric Association. (1980). *The diagnostic and statistical manual of mental disorders* (3rd ed.). Washington, DC: Author.

American Psychiatric Association. (2004). *The diagnostic and statistical manual of metnal disorders* (5th ed.). Washington, DC: Author.

Angel, L. (1949). Constitution in female obesity. *American Journal of Physical Anthropology, 7,* 433–471.

Antczak, J. (1983, February 4). Domestic news. Associated Press. Retrieved December 1, 2005, from LexisNexis Executive database.

Appadurai, A. (1997). *Modernity at large: Cultural dimensions of globalization.* Minneapolis: University of Minnesota Press.

Appleyard, B. (1997, December 28). The end of everything. *Sunday Times.* Retrieved December 1, 2005, from LexisNexis Executive database.

Atkinson, P., & Silverman, D. (1997). Kundera's *Immortality*: The interview society and the invention of the self. *Qualitative Inquiry, 3,* 304–325.

Bakhtin, M. (1981). *The dialogic imagination.* Austin: University of Texas Press.

Bakhtin, M. (1986). *Speech genres and other late essays.* Austin: University of Texas Press.

*Baltimore Sun.* (1996, October 10). Live. Retrieved July 15, 2002, from LexisNexis Executive database.

Bateson, G., Jackson, D., Haley, J., & Weakland, J. (1957). Toward a theory of schizophrenia. *Behavioral Science, 1,* 251–264.

Behar, R. (1996). *The vulnerable observer: Anthropology that breaks your heart.* New York: Beacon Press.

Bemis, K. (1978). Current approaches to the etiology and treatment of anorexia nervosa. *Psychological Bulletin, 85*(3), 593–617.

# References

Blackman, L. (1999). An extraordinary life: The legacy of an ambivalence. *New Formations, 36*, 111–124.

Blackman, L., & Walkerdine, V. (2000). *Mass hysteria: Critical psychology and media studies*. London: Macmillan.

Boone-O'Neill, C. (1982). *Starving for attention*. Crossroads Publishings.

Bordo, S. (1993). *The unbearable weight: Feminism, Western culture, and the body*. Berkeley: University of California Press.

Bordo, S. (1997). *Twilight zones: The hidden life of cultural images from Plato to O. J.* Berkeley: University of California Press.

Bordowitz, G. (1994). Dense moments. In Sappington, R., & Stallings, T. (Eds.). *Uncontrollable bodies: Testimonies of identity and culture* (pp. 25–44). Seattle, WA: Bay Press.

Botta, R. A. (1999). Television images and adolescent girls' body image disturbances. *Journal of Communication, 49*, 22–41.

Braidotti, R. (1997). In the sign of the feminine: Reading Diana. *Theory & Event, 1*(4). Available at: http://muse.jhu.edu/journals/theory_and_event/v001/1.4braidotti.html

Bray, A. (1996). Anorexic bodies: Reading disorder. *Cultural Studies, 10*(3), 413–429.

Brown, M. (1995, December 3). I hold their hands and talk, but I don't wear a uniform or anything; Diana opens her heart on trips to comfort dying. *Sunday Mirror*. Retrieved December 1, 2005, from LexisNexis Executive database.

Bruch, H. (1939a). Obesity in childhood I: Physical growth and development of obese children. *American Journal of Diseases of Children, 58*(3), 457–484.

Bruch, H. (1939b). Obesity in childhood II: Basal metabolism and serum cholesterol of obese children. *American Journal of Diseases of Children, 58*(4), 1001–1022.

Bruch, H. (1952). *Don't be afraid of your child*. New York: Farrar, Strauss and Young.

Bruch, H. (1957). *The importance of overweight*. New York: W.W. Norton.

Bruch, H. (1961a). The effects of modern psychiatric theories on our society—a psychiatrist's view. *Journal of Existential Psychiatry, 2*, 213–232.

Bruch, H. (1961b). Transformation of oral impulses in eating disorders: A conceptual approach. *Psychiatric Quarterly, 35*, 458–481.

Bruch, H. (1973). *Eating disorders: Obesity, anorexia and the person within*. New York: Basic Books.

Bruch, H. (1974). Perils of behavior modification in treatment of anorexia nervosa. *Journal of American Medical Association, 230*, 1419–1422.

Bruch, H. (1978). *The golden cage: The enigma of anorexia nervosa*. Cambridge, MA: Harvard University Press.

Bruch, H., & Touraine, G. (1940). Obesity in childhood V: The family frame of obese children. *Psychosomatic Medicine, 11*(2), 141–206.

# References

Brumberg, J. (1988). *Fasting girls. The history of anorexia nervosa.* Cambridge, MA: Harvard University Press.

Bunym, C. (1987). *The holy feast and holy fast: The religious significance of food to medieval women.* Berkeley: University of California Press.

Burns, M. (2004). Eating like an ox: Femininity and dualistic constructions of bulimia and anorexia. *Feminism & Psychology, 14*(2), 269–295.

Butler, J. (1990). *Gender trouble.* New York: Routledge.

Campbell, B. (1995, November 23). The princess and the pain. *Guardian.* Retrieved December 1, 2005, from LexisNexis Executive database.

Cesno, F., Darrow, S., Bittermann, J., O'Connor, E., Blankley, T., & Morton, B. (1997, August 31). Remembering Princess Diana. CNN. Retrieved December 1, 2005, from LexisNexis Executive database.

Chang, V., & Christakis, N. (2002). Medical modeling of obesity: A transition from action to experience in a 20th century American medical textbook. *Sociology of Health and Illness, 24*(2), 151–177.

Chernin, K. (1981). *The obsession: Reflections on the tyranny of slenderness.* New York: Harper & Row.

Chopra, D. (1993). *Ageless body, timeless mind.* New York: Random House.

Clifford, J. (1986). On ethnographic allegory. In James Clifford & George Marcus. (Eds.), *Writing culture: The politics and poetics of ethnography* (pp. 98–121). Berkeley: University of California Press.

Clifford, J. (1997). *Routes: Travel and translation in the late twentieth century.* Cambridge: Harvard University Press.

Clifford, J., & Marcus, G. (Eds.). (1986). *Writing culture: The politics and poetics of ethnography.* Berkeley: University of California Press.

Clough, P. (1997). Autotelecommunication and autoethnography: A reading of Carolyn Ellis's *Final Negotiations. Sociological Quarterly, 38*(1), 95–110.

Clough, P. (2000). *Autoaffection: Unconscious thought in the age of teletechnology.* Minneapolis: University of Minnesota Press.

Colebrook, C., & Bray, A. (1998). The haunted flesh: Corporeal feminism and the politics of (dis)embodiment. *Signs, 24*(1), 35–68.

Curry, A., & Lauer, M. (2004, December 6). Videotaped conversation between Princess Diana and Peter Settelen. NBC. Retrieved December 1, 2005, from LexisNexis Executive database.

Davis, K. (1995). *Reshaping the female body: The dilemma of cosmetic surgery.* New York: Routledge.

Dean, M. (1994). *Critical and effective histories: Foucault's method and historical sociology.* London: Routledge.

Deleuze, G. (1988). Foldings, or the inside of thought (subjectivation). In G. Deleuze, *Foucault* (pp. 94–123). Minneapolis: University of Minnesota Press.

# References

Deleuze, G., & Guattari, F. (1987). *A thousand plateaus: Capitalism and schizophrenia*. Minneapolis: University of Minnesota Press.

Deleuze, G. (1992). Postscript on the societies of control. *October*, Winter, 3–7.

Denzin, N. (1992). The many faces of emotionality. Reading Persona. In C. Ellis & M. Flaherty (Eds.), *Investigating subjectivity. Research on lived experience* (pp. 17–30). Newbury Park: Sage.

Denzin, N. (1997). *Interpretive ethnography: Ethnographic practices for the 21st century*. London: Sage.

Denzin, N. (2002).The cinematic society and the reflexive interview. In J. Gubrium & J. Holstein (Eds.), *Handbook of interview research* (pp. 833–848). London: Sage.

Dickinson, C. (1996, October 24). Not even close to Karen at her best. *St. Louis Post-Dispatch*. Retrieved December 1, 2005, from LexisNexis Executive database.

Donaldson, S. (1969). *The suburban myth*. New York: Columbia University Press.

Drury, P., & Nairn, J. (1997, August 31). Goodbye my love; Together to the end . . . the tragic lovers; Princess Diana and her lover Dodi Fayed died after horror car crash in Paris early this morning. *Sunday Mail*. Retrieved December 1, 2005, from LexisNexis Executive database.

Echols, A. (1989). *Daring to be bad: Radical feminism in America, 1967–1975*. Minneapolis: University of Minnesota Press.

Eckermann, L. (1997). Foucault, embodiment and gendered subjectivities: The case of voluntary self-starvation. In A. Petersen & R. Bunton, (Eds.), *Foucault, health and medicine* (pp. 151–169). New York: Routledge.

Ehrenreich, B. (1989). *Fear of falling: The inner life of the middle class*. New York: Pantheon.

Ellis, C., & Bochner, A. (1992). Telling and performing personal stories: The constraints of choice in abortion. In C. Ellis, & M. Flaherty (Eds.), *Investigating subjectivity. Research on lived experience* (pp. 79–101). Newbury Park: Sage.

Ellis, C., & Bochner, A. (2000). Autoethnography, personal narrative, reflexivity: Researcher as subject. In N. K. Denzin, & Y. Lincoln, (Eds.), *Handbook of qualitative research*. (2nd ed., pp. 733–768). Thousand Oaks, CA: Sage.

Evans, J., Rich, E., Holroyd, R. (2004). Disordered eating and disordered schooling: What schools do to middle class girls. *British Journal of Sociology of Education*, 25, (2), 123–142.

Felski, R. (1995). *The gender of modernity*. Cambridge: Harvard University Press.

Ferreday, D. (2003). Unspeakable bodies: Erasure, embodiment and the pro-ana community. *International Journal of Cultural Studies*, 6, 277–295.

Foucault, M. (1973). *The order of things: An archaeology of the human sciences*. New York: Vinatge.

# References

Foucault, M. (1978). *History of Sexuality: Volume 1. An Introduction.* New York: Vintage Books.

Foucault, M. (1982). Afterword: The subject and power. In H. Dreyfus & P. Rabinow, *Michel Foucault: Beyond structuralism and hermeneutics* (pp. 208–226). Chicago, IL: University of Chicago Press.

Foucault, M. (1984a). What is Enlightenment? In P. Rabinow (Ed.) *The Focault reader* (pp. 32–50). New York: Pantheon.

Foucault, M. (1984b). Nietzsche, genealogy, history. In P. Rabinow (Ed.), *The Foucault reader* (pp. 76–100). New York: Pantheon.

Foucault, M. (1985a). *History of sexuality: Volume 2. The use of pleasure.* New York: Vintage Books.

Foucault, M. (1985b). *History of sexuality: Volume 3. The care of the self.* New York: Vintage Books.

Foucault, M. (1988). The ethic of care for the self as practice of freedom. In James Bernauer & David Rasmussen (Eds.), *The final Foucault* (pp. 1–17). Cambridge, MA: MIT Press.

Fox, N., Ward, K. & O'Rourke, A. (2005). Pro-anorexia, weight-loss drugs and the Internet: An "anti-recovery" explanatory model of anorexia. *Sociology of Health and Illness, 27*(7), 944–971.

Fraad, H. (1990). Anorexia nervosa: The female body as a site of gender and class transition. *Rethinking Marxism, 3*(3–4), 79–99.

Frank, A. (1995). *The wounded story-teller: Body, illness and ethics.* Chicago, IL: University of Chicago Press.

Fromm, E. (1965). *Escape from freedom.* New York: Avon Books. (Original work published in 1941)

Fromm-Reichmann, F. (1940). Notes on the mother rôle in the family group. *Bulletin of the Menninger Clinic, 4*(5), 132–148.

Garfinkel, P. E., Kline, S. A. & Stancer, H. C. (1973). Treatment of anorexia nervosa using operant conditioning techniques. *Journal of Nervous and Mental Disease, 157*(6), 428–433.

Garner, D., Garfinkel, P., Schwartz, D., & Thompson, M. (1980). Cultural expectations of thinness in women. *Psychological Reports, 47,* 483–491.

Garrett, C. (1999). *Beyond anorexia: Narrative, spirituality and recovery.* Cambridge: Cambridge University Press.

Garrison, F. (1922). History of endocrine doctrine. In L. Barker & D. LL. (Eds.), *Endocrinology and metabolism* (pp. 45–74). New York: D. Appleton and Co.

Giddens, A. (1991). *Modernity and self-identity: Self and society in the late modern age.* Stanford, CA: Stanford University Press.

Giles Banks, C. (1992). "Culture" in culture-bound syndromes: The case of anorexia nervosa. *Social Science and Medicine, 34*(8), 867–884.

Gilligan, C. (1982). *In a different voice: Psychological theory and women's development.* Cambridge, MA: Harvard University Press.

Goulding, J. (1983, February 4). Domestic News. *United Press International.* Retrieved December 1, 2005, from LexisNexis Executive database.

Grant, S. (1996). *The passion of Alice.* New York: Bantam.

Gremillion, H. (1992). Psychiatry as social ordering: Anorexia nervosa, a paradigm. *Social Science and Medicine, 35*(1), 57–71.

Gremillion, H. (2003). *Feeding anorexia: Gender and power at a treatment center.* Durham, NC: Duke University Press.

Grob, G. (1984). *Mental illness and American society, 1875–1940.* Princeton: Princeton University Press.

Grob, G. (1991). *From asylum to community: Mental health policy in modern America.* Princeton: Princeton University Press.

Gubrium, J., & Holstein, J. (2002). From the individual interview to the interview society. In J. Gubrium & J. Holstein (Eds.), *Handbook of interview research: Context and method* (pp. 3–33). Thousand Oaks: Sage.

Hacking, I. (1995). *Rewriting the soul: Multiple personality and the sciences of memory.* Princeton, NJ: Princeton University Press.

Halmi, K. A., Agras, W. S., Crow, S., Mitchell, J., Wilson, G. T., Bryson, S. W., Kraemer, H.C. (2005). Predictors of treatment acceptance and completion in anorexia nervosa: Implications for future study designs. *Archives of General Psychiatry, 62*(7), 76–81.

Halmi, K., Powers, P., & Cunningham, S. (1973). Treatment of anorexia nervosa with behavior modification. *Archives of General Psychiatry, 32,* 93–96.

Haraway, D. (1997). *Modest_Witness@Second_Millenium.FemaleMan©_Meets_Onco Mouse™. Feminism and technoscience.* London: Routledge.

Harrison, K. (2000). The body electric: Thin-ideal media and eating disorders in adolescents. *Journal of Communication, 50,* 119–143.

Hatch-Bruch, J. (1996). *Unlocking the golden cage: An intimate biography of Hilde Bruch M.D.* Carlsbad, CA: Gürze Books.

Hepp, U., Spindler, A., & Milos, G. (2005). Eating disorder symptomatology and gender role orientation. *International Journal of Eating Disorders, 37*(3); 227–233.

Henriques, J., Hollway, W., Urwin, C., Venn, C., & Walkerdine, V. (Eds.). (1984). *Changing the subject: Psychology, social regulation and subjectivity.* London: Methuen.

Hepworth, J. (1999). *The social construction of anorexia nervosa.* London: Sage.

Hermans, H., & Kempen, H. (1993). *The dialogic self: Meaning as movement.* New York: Academic Press.

Herzog, D. B., Dorer, D. J., Keel, P. K., Selwyn, S. E., Ekeblad, E. R., Flores, A. T., et al. (1999). Recovery and relapse in anorexia and bulimia nervosa: A 7.5-year follow-up study. *Journal of American Academy of Child and Adolescent Psychiatry*, *38*(7), 829–837.

Hilgartner, S. (2004). Mapping systems and moral order: Constituting property in genome laboratories. In S. Jasanoff (Ed.), *States of knowledge: The co-production of science and social order* (pp. 131–141). London: Routledge.

Hoerburger, R. (1996, October 13). In 1979, Karen Carpenter, the Little Bo Peep of pop, made a racy solo album, her brother tried to suppress it. Last week, he gave in. *Observer*. Retrieved December 1, 2005, from LexisNexis Executive database.

Horsfall, J. (1991). The silent participant: Bryan Turner on anorexia nervosa. *Australian and New Zealand Journal of Sociology*, *27*(2), 232–234.

Hoskins, M., & Leseho, J. (1996). Changing metaphors of the self: Implications for counseling. *Journal for Counseling & Development*, *74*, 243–252.

Huyssen, A. (1986). Mass culture as woman: Modernism's other. In T. Modleski (Ed.), *Studies in entertainment: Critical approaches to mass culture* (pp. 188–208). London: Routledge.

Jackson, M. (1998). *Minima ethnographica: Intersubjectivity and the anthropological project*. Chicago, IL: University of Chicago Press.

Jasanoff, S. (2004). Ordering knowledge, ordering society. In S. Jasanoff (Ed), *States of knowledge: The co-production of science and social order* (pp. 13–45). London: Routledge.

Jimenez, M. A. (1993). Psychiatric conceptions of mental disorder among immigrants and African-Americans in nineteenth and early twentieth century American history. *Research in Social Movements, Conflicts and Change*, *16*, 1–33.

Johnson, M. E., Brems. C., & Fischer, P. (1996). Sex role conflict, social desirability, and eating-disorder attitudes and behaviors. *Journal of General Psychology*, *123*(1), 75–87.

Jones, K. (2000). *Living between danger and love: The limits of choice*. New Brunswick, NJ: Rutgers University Press.

Kempley, R. (1989, January 26). Drama of the dolls; "Superstar's" riveting Carpenter metaphor. *Washington Post*. Retrieved December 1, 2005, from LexisNexis Executive database.

Kiesinger, C. (1998). From interview to story: Writing Abbie's life. *Qualitative Inquiry*, *4*(1), 71–95.

King, S. (In press). Pink Ribbons Inc.: The emergence of cause-related marketing and the corporatization of the breast cancer movement. In L. Reed & P. Saukko (Eds.), *Governing the female body: Gender health and networks of power.* Albany: State University of New York Press.

Kirkland, K. (1987). *Dancing on my grave*. New York: Doubleday.

Kraut, A. (1994). *Silent travelers: Germs, genes and the "immigrant menace."* New York: Basic Books.

Lather, P. (1993). Fertile obsessions: Validity after poststructuralism. *Sociological Quarterly, 34*(4), 673–693.

Lester, R. (1997). The (dis)embodied self in anorexia nervosa. *Social Science and Medicine, 44*(4), 479–489.

Lowney, K., & Holstein, J. (2000). Victims, villains and talk-show selves. In J. Gubrium & J. Holstein (Eds.), *Troubled identities in a postmodern world* (pp. 23–45). Oxford: Oxford University Press.

MacSween, M. (1993). *Anorexic bodies: A feminist and sociological perspective on anorexia nervosa.* New York: Routledge.

Mahowald, M. B. (1992). To be or not to be a woman: Anorexia nervosa, normative gender roles, and feminism. *Journal of Medicine and Philosophy, 17,* 233–251.

Maisel, R., Epston, D., & Borden, A. (2004). *Biting the hand that starves you: Inspiring resistance to eating disorders.* New York: W.W. Norton.

Malson, H. (1998). *The thin woman: Feminism, post-structuralism and the social psychology of anorexia nervosa.* London: Routledge.

Malson, H., Finn, D. M., Treasure, J., Clarke, S., & Anderson, G. (2004). Constructing the "eating disordered patient": A discourse analysis of accounts of treatment experiences. *Journal of Community and Applied Psychology, 14,* 473–489.

Marcus, G. (1986). Contemporary problems of ethnography in the modern world system. In James Clifford & George Marcus (Eds.), *Writing culture: The politics and poetics of ethnography* (pp. 165–193). Berkeley: University of California Press.

Marcus, G. (1998). *Ethnography through thick and thin.* Princeton: Princeton University Press.

Martin, E. (1994). *Flexible bodies: The role of immunity in American culture from the days of polio to the age of AIDS.* Boston: Beacon Press.

McNeill, M. (1993). Dancing with Foucault: Feminism and power-knowledge. In C. Ramazanoglu (Ed.), *Up against Foucault: Explorations of some tensions between Foucault and feminism* (pp. 147–178). New York: Routledge.

Mead, M. (1954). Review of the book *Don't be afraid of your child. American Journal of Orthopsychiatry, 24,* 426–429.

Millar, H. R., Wardell, F., Vyvyan, J. P., Naji, S. A., Prescott, G. J., Eagles, J. M. (2005). Anorexia nervosa mortality in northeast Scotland, 1965–1999. *American Journal of Psychiatry, 162*(4), 753-757.

Miller, P., & O'Leary, T. (1994). Governing the calculable Person. In A. Hopwood & P. Miller (Eds.), *Accounting as social and institutional practice* (pp. 265-289). Cambridge; Cambridge University Press.

Minh-Ha, T. (1989). *Woman, native, other: Writing postcoloniality and feminism*. Bloomington: Indiana University Press.

Mintz, S., & Kellogg, S. (1988). *Domestic revolutions: A social history of American family life*. New York: Free Press.

Morton, T. (1993). *Diana—Her true story*. New York: Simon & Schuster.

Moulding, N. (2003). Constructing the self in mental health practice: Identity, individualism and the feminization of deficiency. *Feminist Review*, 75, 57-74.

Mukai, T. (1988). A call for our language: Anorexia from within. *Women's Studies International Forum*, 12(6), 613–638.

Mulveen, R., & Hepworth, J. (2006). An interpretive phenomenological analysis of participation in a pro-anorexia Internet site and its relationship with disordered eating, *Journal of Health Psychology*, 11(2), 283–296.

Myers, P., & Riocca, F. (1992). The elastic body image. The effect of television advertising and programming on body image distortions in young women. *Journal of Communication*, 42(3), 108–133.

netdoctor. co. uk (2007). *Largactil*. Accessed September 12th, 2007. http://www.netdoctor.co.uk/medicines/100001461.html

O'Connor, J. (1988, December, 31). A success story's unhappy ending. *New York Times*. Retrieved December 1, 2005, from LexisNexis Executive database.

Orbach, S. (1986). *Hunger strike: The anorectic's struggle as a metaphor for our age*. New York: Norton.

Parsons, T. (2004, March 8). Put a cork in Di's vintage whines. *The Mirror*. Retrieved December 1, 2005, from LexisNexis Executive database.

Patton, Q. (2002). *Qualitative research & evaluation methods*. London: Sage.

Persaud, R. (1995, November 22). Did Diana's childhood set her forever on the brink? A top psychiatrist examines the Princess's mind. *Daily Mail*. Retrieved December 1, 2005, from LexisNexis Executive database.

Petersen, A., & Bunton, R. (2002). *The new genetics and the public's health*. London: Routledge.

Piaget, J. (1954). *The construction of reality in the child*. New York: Basic Books.

Polkinghorne, D. (1997). Reporting qualitative research as practice. In W. Tierney & Y. Lincoln (Eds.), *Representation and the text: Re-framing the narrative voice* (pp. 3–22). Albany: State University of New York Press.

Pollack, D. (2003). Pro-eating disorder websites: What should be the feminist response? *Feminism and Psychology*, 13, 246–251.

Polsky, A. (1991). *The rise of the therapeutic state*. Princeton: Princeton University Press.

Preble, W. (1915). Obesity and malnutrition. *Boston Medical and Surgical Journal*, 20, 740–744.

Probyn, E. (1987). The anorexic body. In Arthur Kroker & Marilouise Kroker (Eds.), *Body invaders: Panic sex in America* (pp. 201–211). New York: Saint Martin's Press.

Probyn, E. (1993). *Sexing the self. Gendered positions in cultural studies.* New York: Routledge.

Probyn, E. (2000). *Carnal appetites: FoodSexIdentities.* London: Routledge.

Richardson, L. (2000). Writing: A method of inquiry. In N. K. Denzin and Y. S. Lincoln (Eds.) Handbook of quantitative research (2n edition) (pp. 923–948). Thousand Oaks, Sage.

Richardson, L, & St. Pierre, E. A. (2005). Writing: A method of inquiry. In N. K. Denzin & Y. S. Lincoln (Eds.), *The Sage handbook of qualitative research.* (3rd ed., pp. 959–978). Thousand Oaks, CA: Sage.

Riesman, D. (1976). *The lonely crowd: A study of the changing American character.* New Haven: Yale University Press. (Original work published in 1950)

Rich, E. (2006). The anorexic (dis)connection: Managing anorexia as an "illness" and an "identity." *Sociology of Health and Illness, 28*(3), 284–305.

Rimmon-Kennan, S. (2002). *Narrative fiction: Contemporary poetics* (2nd ed.). New York: Routledge.

Robertson, M. (November 24, 2000). Why does it take a celebrity to make an illness interesting? *Sun.* Retrieved December 1, 2005, from LexisNexis executive database.

Ronai, C. R. (1998). Sketching with Derrida: An ethnography of a researcher/erotic dancer, *Qualitative Inquiry, 4*(3), 405–420.

Rose, N. (1984). *The psychological complex: Psychology, politics and society in England 1869-1939.* London: Routledge.

Rose, N. (1996). *Reinventing our selves.* Cambridge: Cambridge University Press.

Rose, N. (1999). *Practices of freedom.* Cambridge: Cambridge University Press.

Rousewell, D. (2004, February 15). Di tried suicide with Charles' knife. *Sunday People.* Retrieved December 1, 2005, from LexisNexis Executive database.

Saukko, P. (1996). Anorexia nervosa: Rereading the stories that became me. *Cultural Studies: A Research Annual, 1,* 49–65.

Saukko, P. (1999). Fat boys and goody girls: Hilde Bruch's work on eating disorders and the American anxiety about democracy, 1930–1960. In Jeffrey Sobal & Donna Maurer (Eds.), *Weighty issues: Constructing fatness and thinness as social problems* (pp. 31–49). Hawthorne, NY: Aldine de Gruyter.

Saukko, P. (2000). Between voice and discourse: Quilting interviews on anorexia. *Qualitative Inquiry, 6*(3), 299–317.

Saukko, P. (2003). *Doing research in cultural studies: An introduction to new and classical methodological approaches.* London: Sage.

Saukko, P. (2005). Methodologies for cultural studies: An integrative approach. In N. K. Denzin & Y. S. Lincoln (Eds.), *The Sage handbook of qualitative research* (pp. 343–356). Thousand Oaks, CA: Sage.

Schwartz, H. (1986). *Never satisfied: A cultural history of diets, fantasies and fat.* New York: Free Press.

Scott, V. (1988, May 25). Actress finds Karen Carpenter role "eerie." United Press International. Retrieved December 1, 2005, from LexisNexis Executive database.

Sheldon, W. (1940). *The varieties of human physique: An introduction to constitutional psychology.* New York: Harpers.

Sheldon, W. (1942). *The varieties of temperament: A psychology of constitutional difference.* New York: Harpers.

Skolnick, A. (1991). *Embattled paradise: The American family in the age of uncertainty.* New York: Basic Books.

Snitow, A. (1992). Feminism and motherhood: An American reading. *Feminist Review, 40,* 32–51.

Spitzack, C. (1993). The spectacle of anorexia nervosa. *Text and Performance Quarterly, 13*(1), 1–20.

Stearns, P. (1997). *Fat history: Bodies and beauty in the modern west.* New York: New York University Press.

Steptoe, A., Doherty, S., Rink, E., Kerry, S., Kendrick, T., & Hilton, S. (1999). Behavioural counselling in general practice for the promotion of healthy behaviour among adults at increased risk of coronary heart disease: Randomised trial. *British Medical Journal,* 319(7215), 943–947.

Susman, W. (1989). Did success spoil the United States? Dual representations in post-war America. In L. May (Ed.), *Recasting America: Culture and politics in the age of Cold War* (pp. 19–37). Chicago: University of Chicago Press.

Thompson, B. (1994). *A hunger so wide and so deep: American women speak out on eating problems.* Minneapolis: University of Minnesota Press.

Volosinov, V. (1973). *Marxism and the philosophy of language.* New York: Seminar Press.

Walkerdine, V. (1988). *Counting girls out.* London: Virago.

Walkerdine, V. (1993). Beyond developmentalism? *Theory & Psychology, 3*(4), 451–469.

Walkerdine, V. (1999). The crowd in the age of Diana: Ordinary inventiveness and the popular imagination. In A. Kear & D. L. Steinberg (Eds.), *Mourning Diana: Nation, culture and the performance of grief* (pp. 98–107). London: Routledge.

Walkerdine, V., Lucey, H., & Melody, J. (2001). *Growing up girl: Psychosocial explorations of gender and class*. London: Palgrave.

Walters, S. (1992). *Lives together/worlds apart: Mothers and daughters in popular culture*. Berkeley: University of California Press.

Way, K. (1995). "Never too rich . . . or too thin: The role of stigma in the social construction of anorexia nervosa. In Donna Maurer & Jeffrey Sobal (Eds.), *Eating agendas: Food and nutrition as social problems* (pp. 91–116). New York: Aldine de Gruyter.

Weiss, N. (1977). Mother, the invention of necessity: Dr. Benjamin Spock's *Baby and Child Care, American Quarterly*, 29(5), 517–546.

White, M., & Epston, D. (1990). *Narrative means to therapeutic ends*. New York: W.W. Norton & Company.

Wiseman, C., Gray, J., Mosimann, J., & Ahrens, A. (1990). Cultural expectations of thinness in women: An update. *International Journal of Eating Disorders*, 11, 85–89.

Wolfenstein, M. (1951). Fun morality: An analysis of recent American child-training literature. *Journal of Social Issues*, 7(4), 15–25.

Wooley, S. (1994). Sexual abuse and eating disorders: The concealed debate. In P. Fallon, M. Katzman, & S. Wooley (Eds.), *Feminist perspectives on eating disorders* (pp. 171–211). New York: The Guilford Press.

Wrottersley, C. (1995, December 13). Hooked on Di's helping habit; compulsion that drives do-gooders; compulsive helpers may be suffering from the Diana Syndrome. *Daily Mirror*. Retrieved December 1, 2005, from LexisNexis Executive database.

Wykes, M., & Gunther, B. (2005). *The media & body image: If looks could kill*. London: Sage.

# Index

accent, social accents, 6; multiple accents in intrapersonal and political discourses, 110–112
achievement, and anorexia, 9, 17, 24–25; Crystal's story, 88–89; Jeanne's story, 86, a more nuanced interpretation of empowering and disempowering aspects, 98, 105, 108; and perfectionism in narrative therapy, 102–103; problems in narrative therapy's view on achievement/perfectionism, 103; problematic features of theories of anorexia as resulting from high achievement/perfectionism, 27–29; Taru's story, 86–87; women interviewed as high achievers, 85
adaptability, *see* flexible self
Adorno, T., 8, 50
Al-Fayed, Dodi (Princess Diana's lover), 64
Ahrens, A., 59
Angel, L., 41
alienation, of anorexics in relation to descriptions of the conditions, 1, 9, 82, 90
anorexic/bulimic voice, 101–103
Antczak, J., 64–65
Associated Press (AP), 64
Appadurai, A., 108
Appleyard, B., 71
Atkinson, P., 80
authenticity, *See* true self
authoritarian personality, 50
autoethnography, 9, 12, 17, 34–35, 113
authorial position, 13
autonomous self, critique of anorexics as nonautonomous or weak in Taru's story, 91–92; the empowering and disempowering sides of the conception of women with eating disorders as nonautonomous, 96–98; ideal of, 1, 4, 5, 6, 9, 10, 39, 50–51, 54–55, 57, 75–76, 99, 107–108, 111; and Karen Carpenter, 64–69, 81; reflection on the empowering and disempowering aspects of autonomy in Eleanora's story, 92–94; wanting to be autonomous, Eleanora's story, 88

Bakhtin, M., 2, 12, 83, 97, 104
ballet, dancing and anorexia, 86–87
*Baltimore Sun*, 68
Barbie: Barbie animation, 66–67
beauty ideals, critique of feminist criticism, 61, 80; gendered contradictions articulated by, 4, 7, 59, 105–106; research on eating disorders as too focused on, 33, 90; slender, 1, 8, 9, 18, 23, 27, 51, 57, 59
Behar, R., 79
behavior modification, 9; autoethnography, 19–22
Bird, J., 103
Blackman, L., 51, 58, 62, 72
Blair, Tony (UK Prime Minister), 63
Bochner, A., 79
body image, distorted, 18
Boone-O'Neill, C., 33
Borden, A., 11, 101–106
Borderline Personality Disorder, and Princess Diana, 70
Bordo, S., 1, 2, 3, 7, 33, 54, 59, 61, 76, 80, 81, 106–107
Bordowitz, G., 12, 33
both/and logic, 6–7, 61, 98, 111–112
Botta, R.A., 59
Braidotti, R., 73, 76
Bray, A., 1, 5, 51, 60, 61, 67, 73, 89
Brems, C., 4

# Index

Brown, M., 71
Bruch, H., 3, 6, 9, 13, 24, 27, 29, 57, 63, 65, 76, 106, 108; critical analysis of work, 37–55, 81
Brumberg, J., 3, 4, 17, 37, 39, 47
Bunym, C., 17
Bunton, R., 53, 107
Burns, M., vii, 63
Bush, George W. (American President), 111
Butler, J., 2, 27

Campbell, B., 70
Carpenter, K. 3, 8, 10–11, 13, 54, 97; analysis of news coverage, 64–69
celebrities, and identification, 62
Cesno, F., 72
Chang, V., 42, 45, 52
character work, in Crystal's story, 95
Charles, Prince, 58, 70, 75
Chernin, K., 2, 3, 59
choice, anorexia as, 60
Chopra, D., 96
Christakis, N., 42, 45, 52
Christians, C., vii
Clifford, J., 78, 106
Clough, P., 80
Cold War, 49
Cole, C.L., vii
Colebrook, C., 60, 61
Communism, fear of, 8, 10, 49, 51
consciousness, false 2, 6, 60; polyvocal, 6, 110–111
Conservatism, anorexics being informed by 7, 10, 52, 58, 67, 76; and "family values," 62, 76; and femininity, 67; Jeanne's story on anorexia, 86–87
coproduction, 107
Cunningham, S., 20
Curry, A., 74

Darwinism, social Darwinism, 75
Davis, K., 33, 61, 81
Dean, James (actor), 49
Dean, N., 38
Deleuze, G., 61, 112–113
Denzin, N., vii, and texts constructing subjects, 17; and cinematic interview, 78, 83, 97
Dexedrin, 42
*Diagnostic and Statistical Manual of Mental Disorders* (DSM), 3, 37, 54

dialogic theory, 2, 6–7, 83
Diana, Princess, 10, 13, 23, 97; news coverage of, 70–75, 103
dichotomies underlying definitions and treatment of eating disorders, 2, 7, 52, 60, 73, 99, 108
Dickinson, C., 69
disco-music, 68
discourse analysis, 13
Donaldson, S., 49

Eckermann, L., 61
either/or logic, 61, 98, 111–112
Ellis, C., 79
emotional sociology, 79
endocrinological theory of obesity, 39, 40–41
Epston, D., 11, 101–106
eugenics, 9, 41, 46
Evans, J., 103
experience, researcher's access to, 81–82
externalization, in narrative therapy, 101

false consciousness, *see* consciousness, false
family, dysfunctional causing anorexia, 18, 29, 47–50, 67; dysfunction causing obesity, 44–47
fascism, 10, 49, 51
father, ineffectual father, 18, 45, 51; autoethnography, 30–33
Felski, R., 7, 51
femininity, *see* gender identity, normal, 2, 51–52
feminist research, and autobiography, 78–79; and being faithful to women's voices, 77; on contradictions articulated by slender beauty ideals, 3–4, 59; on eating disorders, 3, 26, 54, 63; patronizing towards anorexics, 60; and political nature of anorexia, 4, 106–107; on problematic nature of discourses on eating disorders, 2, 5, 54
Finland, 8; stage of autoethnography, 15–35
Fischer, P., 4
fitness, and treatment of eating disorders, 2; and strength, 5, 108
flexible self, and Crystal's story, 96–97; flexible/adaptable self, 3, 8, 10, 57, 99, 103, 111; and Princess Diana, 70–75
Foucault, M., 7, 17, 22, 24, 38–39, 61–62, 80, 82, 89–90, 101, 107, 112

# Index

Fox, N., 5, 60, 82
Fraad, H., 27
Frankfurt School, 8, 47, 52, 108
Froehlich's syndrome, 39, 42
Fromm, E., 47–48, 50
Fromm-Reichmann, F., 47–48, 110

Garfinkel, P., 59
Garfinkel, P.E., 20
Garner, D., 59
Garrett, C., 33
Garrison, F., 42
gender identity, disorder, 4, 9, 18, 51; femininity as valuable, 70, 73, 76; feminist research on denying gender, 26, 80–81; limiting nature, 51; normal or healthy, 1–2, 21, 26–27; as pleasing/directed towards others, 3, 50–53, 71, 72; research on eating disorders as too focused on, 90
genealogy, 38–39, 112
genetics, *see* hereditary theories of obesity
Giddens, A., 106
Giles Banks, C., 17
Gilligan, C., 55
Grant, S., 33
Gremillion, H., 2, 5, 7, 20, 27, 40, 54, 102, 106–107
Grob, G., 44, 47
Grossberg, L., vii
*Guardian* (UK newspaper), 70
Guattari, F., 112–113
Gubrium, J., 78
Gunter, B., 57, 59

Hacking, I., 80
Halmi, K.A., 1, 20
Haraway, D., 12
Harrison, K., 23
Harry, Prince, 75
Hatch-Bruch, J., 40
Haynes, Todd (film director), 63, 66–67
healthy self, 3, 58, 100, 103
Henriques, J., 100
Hepp, U., 4
Hepworth, J., 5, 37, 60, 103
hereditary theories of obesity, 41, 53
Hermans, H., 6, 11, 100, 104–106
Herzog, D.B., 33
Hilgartner, S., 108

historical research, 13
HIV, and Princess Diana, 10, 73
Hoerburger, R., 68
Holroyd, R., 103
Holstein, J., 78, 80
Horkheimer, M., 8
Horsfall, J., 30
Hoskins, M., 100–101
Huyssen, A., 7, 51
hysteria, 71, 74
hygienist, social hygienist notions of obesity, 45–46

immigrants, and obesity, 9, 40–47, 55, 108
immigration policy, 41, 55, 108
individualism, American ideal, 8, 40, 51, 53–55, 69, 108
interview, new forms of interviewing, 77–98

Jackson, M., 79
Jasanoff, S., 3, 11, 100, 107
Jimenez, M.A., 41
Johnson, M.E., 4
Jones, K., 79

Kellogg, S., 46
Kempen, H., 6, 11, 100, 104–106
Kempley, R., 66
Kiesinger, C., 79–81
King, S., 70
Kirkland, K., 33
Kline, S.A., 20
Kraut, A., 41

Largactil, 20
Lather, P., 97
Lauer, M., 74
layered account, 11, 33, 77–98, 112
Leseho, J., 100–101
Lester, R., 89
Levenkron, S., 63
LexisNexis database, 63
Liberal feminism, 52, 69
low culture, *see* mass culture
Lowney, K., 80
Lucey, H., 103

Mahowald, M.B., 27
Maisel, R., 11, 101–106

# Index

Malson, H., vii, 1, 5, 6, 59, 82, 89, 93, 104, 105
Marcus, G., 3, 78, 100, 108
Markula, H., vii
Martin, E., 75
mass culture, 3, 108; as feminine, 3, 7, 51–52; and Karen Carpenter, 64–69
McNeill, M., 5, 54
Mead, M., 47
media, and eating disorders, 22–23, 57–76; and thin body ideals, 1, 23–26, 51, 54, 57–62, 65
Melody, J., 103
methodology, autoethnography, 34–35; framing this book, 6–8; genealogy, 38–39; interviewing, 77–98; layered account, 77–98; space-based VS time-based methodology for studying eating disorders, 100–113
middle-class: anorexia articulating aspiration to middle-class status, women interviewed, 85; anorexia as a middle-class condition, 4, 8, 10, 49, 51, 65; critique of anorexics as wealthy and spoilt in Taru's story, 92; Jeanne's story as telling about, 90–91; problems and insights in the conception of anorexics as middle-class or spoilt, 95–98
Millar, H.R., 33
Miller, D., 46
Milos, G., 4
Minh-Ha, T., 12, 33–34, 83
Minz, S., 46
*Mirror* (UK newspaper), 74
moral theories of obesity, 41, 42, 45
Morton, A., 64
Mosimann, J., 59
mother, overpowering and anorexia, 10, 18, 29–30, 48–49; overpowering and obesity, 43–45
Moulding, N., 2, 5
music, hard/soft rock gendered dichotomy, 64–69
multi-sited ethnography, 8, 11, 108, 112
Mulveen, R. 5, 60
Myers, P., 25, 59

narrative therapy, 6, 100–106, 112
New Age, 75, 96
New Labour, 10–11, 58, 63
Nixon, Richard (US President), 58, 62

obesity, *see* endocrinological theories of obesity, hereditary theories of obesity, moral theories of obesity, psychological theories of obesity, racial theories of obesity
*Observer* (UK newspaper), 68
O'Connor, J., 67
O'Leary, T., 46
Orbach, S., 3, 54, 59, 63, 106
O'Rourke, A., 5, 60, 82
other-directed character, 50–51
outside of the true, anorexics as, 6, 77

*Panorama* (UK TV-programme), 63
Parsons, T., 74
perfectionism, *see* achievement 9, 27–29
Petersen, A., 53, 107
politics, anorexia as informed by conservative politics in Jeanne's story, 86–87; criticism of politicization of eating disorders in Crystal's story, 88–89, 94–95; depoliticized nature of narrative therapy, 103; the empowering and disempowering aspects of viewing eating disorders as political, 96–98; political aspect of anorexia, 4; the political and personal aspects of anorexia, 106–110; political and personal in methodology, 6; politics articulated by discourses on anorexia, 7–8, 52, 55, 76; politics articulated by discourses on obesity, 46–47, 55
Pollack, D., 5, 60
Polsky, A., 46
polyvocal, *see* voices, multiple and consciousness, polyvocal
Powers, P., 20
practice/ontology of the self, anorexia as, 61–62, 89–90; genealogy, 38–39, 112; as a methodology, 17; and subjectivity, 80, 82, 101
Preble, W., 41
prism, research as, 12, 112
pro-ana websites, 5, 60–61, 82
Probyn, E., 1, 5, 51, 61, 67, 79, 99
psychoanalysis, 47
psychological theories of obesity, 45–46, 53–54

quilt, methodological metaphor, 112–113

race, racism informing onset of anorexia, 5; racial theories of obesity, 41–42, 53

# Index

Reagan, Ronald (US President), 58, 62, 86, 90, 96, 111
Reed, L., vii
reductionism, in discourses on anorexia, 25, 33
Rich, E., 5, 6, 60, 82, 93, 103
Richardson, L., 12, 112
Riley, S., vii
religion, informing anorexia, 5; religious understandings of anorexia, 17
Riesman, D., 50–51
Riocca, F., 25, 59
Robertson, M., 23
Ronai, C.R., 33, 34, 77, 82–83, 97, 112
Rose, N., 52, 80
Rousewell, D., 74

Saukko, P., 7
Schizophrenia, Eleanora's story, 87–88
Schwartz, D., 59
Schwarz, H., 40
science and technology studies, 11, 107–108
Scott, V., 66
self, *see* autonomous self, flexible self, healthy self, practice/ontology of the self, true self
self-diagnosis, 17
self-help treatment for eating disorders, 75; Eleanora's story, 89
self-indulgence, anorexics as self-indulgent in Jeanne's story, 91; critique of anorexics as self-indulgent or spoilt in Taru's story, 92; problems and insights in the conception of anorexics as self-indulgent, 95–98
Settelen, Peter (Princess Diana's voicecoach), 73
Shaw, T., 23
Sheldon, W., 41
shyness, and anorexia, 18
Silverman, D., 80
Sixties' counterculture, 65
Skolnick, A., 49
slenderness, *see* beauty ideals
Smurf, 21, 26–27
space-based methodology, 12, 100, 104–106
Spindler, A., 4
Spitzack, C., 25, 106

spoilt, anorexics as *See* middle-class
Stancer, H.C., 20
Stearns, P., 40, 42
Steptoe, A., 25
St. Pierre, E.A., 12
subjectivity, anorexic as object of knowledge, 22; authentic and inauthentic, 60; "folding," as in Deleuze, 61; object/subject dichotomy, 7
suburbia: and mass culture, 49, 58
*Sunday Mail* (UK newspaper), 71
superficial, anorexics as opposed to deep, 67, 69, 81
*Superstar: The Karen Carpenter Story* (film), 66–67
Susman, W., 49
systems, as dominance, 3, 7, 8, 100, 108

talk shows, and methodology coming close to them, 80
Thatcher, Margaret (UK Prime Minister), 57, 63
Thompson, B., 5, 32
Thompson, M., 59
time-based methodology, 12, 100, 104–107
Touraine, G., 44
traditionalism, and obesity, 39, 47, 49, 55; and anorexia, 69
Treichler, P., vii
triangulation, 12
true self, 60–61, stunted in infant feeding, 48–49; ideal in therapy, 100–101

validity, alternative validities in research, 97–98; in research, 12
vanity, and anorexics, 6, 81
Vavrus, M., vii
vegetarianism, and bulimia in Eleanora's story, 88–89
victims, anorexics as, 2, 23, 25, 81; Eleanora's critique of me framing her as a victim, 93; problems embedded in the conception of anorexics as victims, 95–96
voice, multiple voices, 2; methodology sensitive to, 78–80; methodology sensitive to voices and discourses, 82–85; multiple voices in space-based methodology, 100, 104–106, 110–112
Volosinov, V., 2, 6, 82, 100, 110–112

Walkerdine, V., 29, 51, 58, 73, 103
Walstrom, M., vii
war, anorexia and Cold War, 49; anti-war movement and Karen Carpenter, 65; in Cambodia, 66
Ward, K., 5, 60, 82
*Washington Post* (US newspaper), 66–67
Way, K., 57, 62
White, 11, 101

William, Prince, 75
Wiseman, C., 59
working-class, and anorexia, 32–33
Wooley, S., 5
Wrottersley, C., 71
Wykes, M., 57, 59

Xu, H., vii